KINTSUGI MAN

GOD'S POWER TO MEND WHAT'S BROKEN

KINTSUGI MAN

GOD'S POWER TO MEND WHAT'S BROKEN

MCARTHUR L. GLAZE

Kintsugi Man: God's Power to Mend What's Broken

Published by McArthur L. Glaze
106 Ovilla Road, Suite A1, Box 230 Red Oak, Texas 75154
info@mcarthurglaze.com

ISBN: 979-8-9930502-2-5

First Edition 2026
Printed in the United States of America.

DISCLAIMER

This book is designed to provide encouragement, spiritual insight, and general information on the subjects discussed. It is not intended to serve as a substitute for professsional medical, psychological, psychiatric, or therapeutic advice. The author is not a licensed mental health professional, counselor, or therapist. If you or someone you know is experiencing a mental health crisis or requires professional support, please seek the guidance of a qualified professional. The author and publisher assume no responsibility for any actions taken based on the information contained in this book.

DEDICATION

To Adam Dees, you handed me a concept and did not know you were handing me a calling. In one of the small men's gatherings you host, you introduced a room full of men to an ancient artform, and something in my spirit immediately recognized that God had been doing this work in the lives of men long before Japan gave it a name. What you placed in that room became what you are now holding in your hands. I am grateful for your friendship, your leadership, and the moment you pointed a group of men toward something that changed the way I see every broken thing, including myself.

This book exists in part because you created a space where men could encounter truth, and truth found me that day in a way I did not expect. That is the fingerprint of God, and I do not take it lightly.

To every man who has ever picked up the broken pieces of his life and wondered if anything could ever be made of them again.

To the man who is reading these pages in secret because the version of himself the world sees could not afford to be seen holding a book about brokenness.

To the man who bought this with the quiet desperation of someone who has run out of other options.

To the man who has been strong for so long that he has forgotten what it feels like to be honest.

To the young man who is just beginning to understand that the cracks appearing in his life are not the end of his story.

To the older man who has been carrying his fractures for decades and has nearly accepted them as permanent features of who he is.

To every man in between who has loved imperfectly, lost significantly, and tried harder than anyone around him knows, yet still found himself wondering whether God sees anything in him worth saving. He does. He always has. And this book was written to prove it.

To every woman who has loved a broken man and not known what she was looking at. Who has stayed when leaving would have been easier, prayed when silence would have been simpler, and believed in a man who had stopped believing in himself. Your faithfulness has not been invisible to God. What you have carried in love and intercession for the men in your life is part of the golden work He has been doing all along.

This book is for all of you. May the God who repairs broken things with gold meet you in every cracked and honest place these pages touch, and may you never look at fractures the same way again.

TABLE OF CONTENTS

FOREWORD

What McArthur Glaze has written in *Kintsugi Man* is not surface-level inspiration. It is a deeply honest, spiritually grounded invitation for men to face what has been hidden, ignored, and often carried in silence for far too long.

This book speaks to the man behind the image, the one who has learned to function while fractured, to perform while carrying unhealed wounds, and to survive while quietly questioning his own wholeness. McArthur does not shy away from that reality. Instead, he leans into it with courage, clarity, and compassion.

The concept of Kintsugi, repairing what is broken with gold, beautifully reflects the heart of God. Scripture reminds us in 2 Corinthians 4:7 that we carry treasure in earthen vessels. God has never required perfection to release His power. He works through what is cracked, filling broken places with His grace, His truth, and His purpose.

What makes this book so impactful is not only its message but also its authenticity. McArthur writes from a place of lived experience, and you can feel it on every page. His passion for helping men heal, grow, and rediscover their identity is undeniable and contagious.

Personally, this message resonates deeply with me. Growing up in the Bahamas, I never took the time to look inward and address the brokenness I carried. Raised in a single-parent home, exposed to gang activity as a teenager, and experiencing significant loss along the way, I learned early how to survive but not how to heal. It was not until later in life that I began the necessary work of confronting those hidden wounds. That journey has been essential in shaping the man I am today.

Now, as a Pastor and a Red Oak City Councilman, I have the privilege of engaging with men from all walks of life. Whether in my city or as I travel across the country and around the world, I see the same need: men searching for clarity, healing, and purpose. What McArthur presents in this book is a much-needed tool for those who are ready to make sense of their story and step into something greater.

This is more than a book. It is a call to transformation. A call for men to stop hiding, stop performing, and allow God to do His greatest work in the places they once tried to conceal. If you are willing to be honest, this book will meet you there. If you allow it, it will change you.

Ricardo Miller
Pastor and Councilman

INTRODUCTION

THE MAN IN THE MIRROR HAS CRACKS

There is a version of you that nobody has ever met. He lives just beneath the surface of every smile you force at work, every firm handshake, every confident answer you give when someone asks how you are doing. He knows every failure you have never confessed. He carries every wound that never healed the way it should have. He has memorized the weight of every regret, every loss, every moment you fell short of who you believed you were supposed to be. He has been living in silence for years, sometimes decades, and the longer he goes unacknowledged, the heavier everything around you becomes.

And here is what that silence has never been able to change. You are cracked. Not broken beyond use. Not shattered beyond recovery. But cracked, in the specific and undeniable way that a man becomes cracked when life has pressed him hard enough and long enough in the places where he was most vulnerable. The crack is real. It has a history. It has a shape. And it has been there long enough that you have built your entire life around concealing it, performing around it, hoping that if you stay busy enough and productive enough and composed enough, nobody will ever get close enough to see it.

I want to share something that I believe with everything inside of me; something that required me to walk through my own breaking to fully understand. The crack is not the problem. The crack is the invitation. It is the exact place where something more precious than your original wholeness is waiting to be poured in. The God who allowed the crack, the God who, in His sovereignty, permitted the pressure that produced it, has never once looked at the fractured places in your life and seen a man who was finished. He has always seen a man who was being prepared.

Cracks have a way of making themselves known regardless of how hard a man works to conceal them. They show up in the way he responds when he is cornered emotionally. They surface in the patterns that keep repeating in his relationships, no matter how many times he promises himself and the people he loves that this time will be different. They bleed through the performance at three in the morning when the house is quiet, and there is nothing left to distract him from what he has been carrying.

The crack does not disappear because it is ignored. It deepens. And a man who spends his life managing the appearance of a vessel that is quietly fracturing on the inside is a man who is using all of his energy on concealment when God designed that same energy for something infinitely more purposeful.

I know what that concealment costs because I have paid it. I know what it feels like to carry things that have no name, to perform a strength you do not possess, to stand in front of people who believe in you while something on the inside is quietly coming apart. I know the exhaustion of it. I know the loneliness of it.

And I know the moment when the performance finally costs more than it is worth, and something in a man, something that has been waiting a very long time, finally tells the truth. That moment does not feel like strength when it arrives. It feels like a collapse.

But I have learned, in the most personal and most costly way a man can learn something, that what looks like collapse in the life of a surrendered man is very often God clearing the ground to build something that the clutter of performance was never going to allow.

We live in a time when men are disappearing in plain sight. Not dramatically. Not in ways that make headlines or trigger interventions.

They are disappearing quietly, one suppressed emotion at a time, one swallowed truth at a time, one unaddressed wound at a time. They are sitting in offices and sanctuaries and living rooms, surrounded by people, yet feeling a loneliness so complete that they have stopped believing it is possible to be genuinely known. They have been handed a definition of strength by a world that needed them to be productive and were never told that the definition was a lie. Real men do not cry. Real men do not need help. Real men do not look back. And so they buried the grief and the shame and the confusion and the fear beneath layers of achievement and performance and pride, and they have been living on top of that burial ground ever since, wondering why nothing they build ever feels stable, why the ground beneath their lives always seems to be shifting, and why the man in the mirror looks increasingly like a stranger.

The church has not always helped. Men have been handed responsibility without being permitted to be human. They have been told to lead, while nobody asked them how they were doing on the inside. They have sat in pews carrying secret lives that felt too far gone for grace to reach, and they remained silent because the culture of the church, in too many places, communicates more comfort with a man's function than with his fracture. So they performed on Sunday and fractured further on Monday, and eventually many of them stopped showing up at all, not just to church but to their own lives, their marriages, their children, and the purposes God placed inside them before they were born. God, however, has never stopped showing up for them.

Centuries ago in Japan, an artist developed a practice that I believe God allowed to exist as a picture for this very moment in the lives of broken men. When a piece of pottery broke, most people did one of two things: they either threw it away or attempted to hide the damage, gluing the pieces back together and concealing the cracks as best they could so the vessel could pass as whole. But this artist did something that completely overturned both of those instincts. He gathered each broken fragment with extraordinary care. He mixed lacquer with gold, genuine gold, precious, luminous, and impossible to ignore, and he filled every single crack with it. Not to hide what had happened. Not to pretend the vessel had never been broken. But to make the breaking the most visible and most celebrated feature of the finished piece.

What came out of that artist's hands was not a restored version of what the vessel used to be. It was something the vessel could never have become without the breaking. Something more layered, valuable, and more breathtaking than its original form had ever possessed.

The gold did not apologize for being visible. Instead, it announced itself. It caught the light. And every person who looked at that finished piece understood immediately that what made it extraordinary was not that it had survived intact. It was shattered completely and repaired with something more precious than the original material.

That practice is called Kintsugi. It means golden joinery. I want you to sit with the most radical truth buried within that art form because it is the truth this entire book is built upon. The repaired piece is worth more than the original. Not equally valuable. More valuable. The gold does not diminish the vessel. It defines it. The crack is not the tragedy of the story. The crack is where the treasure entered. And the man who stands on the other side of genuine repair, with gold visible in every place he was fractured, is not a lesser version of who he was before the breaking. He is the version that could only exist because of it.

I want you to let that sink in. Because everything the world told you about your cracks was wrong. Every voice that said your wounds disqualified you was wrong. Every conclusion you drew about yourself in the aftermath of your worst seasons, every verdict that told you the broken version of yourself was the final version, was wrong. God has never once looked at a cracked man and seen him as disqualified. He has looked at every fracture in your life and seen exactly what the Kintsugi artist sees when he picks up a broken piece from the floor. Not a failure. Not a waste. A surface waiting for gold.

This is not borrowed inspiration dressed up in Christian language. This is the consistent, documented, and unbroken testimony of God's dealings with broken men throughout Scripture. God has never discarded a broken piece. He has never surveyed the wreckage of a man's failures and concluded that there was nothing left worth saving.

What he does with broken men goes far beyond repair. He transforms them. He fills every crack, every hollow place, every gap carved out by loss, sin, and suffering with something more precious than what occupied that space before. The man who experiences that process does not return to who he was. He becomes something greater. He carries more substance in his scars than he ever carried in his wholeness. The things he spent years trying to hide become the most powerful and golden elements of his story.

I have seen this in Scripture. I have seen it in the lives of men I have walked alongside in ministry. And I have seen it in my own life, in the places where I was most certain the damage was permanent, in the seasons when I could not see any possible purpose for what I was going through, and in the moments when the gap between who I was and who God said I was felt too wide to ever be closed.

The gold is real. The repair is real. And the God who does it is not a distant, theoretical God managing a universe from a comfortable distance. He is the Potter with His hands in the clay, present in the mess, committed to the process, and certain about what the finished piece is going to look like, even when the man inside the process cannot see anything but the breaking.

Let me ask you something. I believe God has been waiting for you to answer honestly, perhaps for years. Not whether you have been broken. Every man reading these words has been broken in some way, in some place, at some point in his story. But what have you done with the broken pieces? Have you buried them? Have you hidden them? Have you medicated them or raged against them? Have you allowed the weight of your fractures to define your ceiling and shrink the boundaries of everything you were created to be? Or, are you ready, perhaps for the very first time, to place those pieces in the hands of the One who can do with them what no human effort, determination, or strategy has ever been sufficient to accomplish?

Second Corinthians 4:7 says that we carry this treasure in earthen vessels, so that the surpassing power belongs to God and not to us. The vessel was never supposed to be the point. The treasure inside it was always the point. God has never needed a perfect vessel to carry perfect power. He has always worked through cracked ones, through the fractured and the overlooked, through those the world had already written off, filling their cracks with a gold so luminous and unmistakable that the only explanation for it was Him.

Your cracks are not your conclusion. They are the canvas. The Artist is ready. The gold is already in His hands. And He has never once looked at a broken piece and seen anything other than the masterpiece it was always destined to become.

Chapter 1

BROKEN BEFORE YOU KNEW YOUR NAME

There are wounds in a man's life that he did not create. Some fractures were present before he ever had the language to describe them, before he ever had the awareness to recognize them, before he ever had the capacity to protect himself from them. Some men spend their entire lives carrying pain they did not choose, living beneath the ceiling of a broken inheritance they never asked to receive, and wondering why nothing they build ever seems to stand the way it should. The answer to that question often does not begin with the man standing in front of the mirror. It begins generations before he was ever born.

I have sat with enough men in enough honest conversations to know that this is one of the most avoided truths in a man's life. It is easier to take full personal responsibility for everything wrong, to own it all as the product of your own choices and failures, than it is to look back at what was handed to you before you were old enough to refuse it. Taking personal responsibility feels like strength.

To most men, looking at what was inherited feels like making excuses. But there is a difference between an excuse and an honest reckoning, and a man who cannot distinguish between the two will spend his entire life either blaming everyone else for his condition or carrying the full weight of a brokenness that was never entirely his to begin with. Neither posture produces healing. Both keep a man stuck in a story that God is trying to rewrite.

The Bible does not soften this reality. Exodus 20:5 speaks plainly about iniquity being visited upon children through the generations of those who came before them. That is not designed to produce fatalism or despair. It is a verse designed to produce honesty because you cannot address what you refuse to acknowledge, and you cannot be free from a chain you have never admitted is wrapped around you. God named the generational pattern not to condemn the son but to confront the cycle, and the first step toward breaking it is being willing to look at it without flinching.

Think about the man who raised you, or the absence of the man who should have. Think about what he taught you without ever opening his mouth, through the way he handled pressure, the way he treated your mother, the way he responded to failure, and the way he either showed up or disappeared when things became difficult.

Boys do not learn manhood from lectures. They absorb it. They watch, they imitate, they internalize, and by the time they are old enough to realize what they have taken in, it has already become the architecture of how they think, feel, and respond to the world. If what they absorbed was healthy, they built on a solid foundation. But if what they absorbed was broken, they begin their adult lives already cracked, already leaning, already carrying weight that was never theirs to carry in the first place.

I want to be specific about the kind of cracking that happens in a boy before he ever becomes a man because generational brokenness is not one thing. It arrives in different forms depending on the home, the history, and the specific fractures that were already present in the men who came before him. Fatherlessness is one of the deepest and most widespread of these fractures, and it does not only mean a physically absent father.

Some of the loneliest boys in the world grew up in the same house as their fathers. They sat at the same dinner table, rode in the same car, lived under the same roof, and still never truly knew the man.

They had a father who was present in body but absent in everything that actually mattered. No affirmation. No honest conversation about what it means to be a man. No safe space to ask questions, admit fear, or process failure. Just silence, performance, or a man too consumed by his own unaddressed wounds to have anything genuine left to give his son.

That kind of absence leaves a particular kind of crack, one that is harder to name because there is no dramatic event to point to, just a slow and quiet emptiness that a boy carries into every relationship, every room, and every challenge for the rest of his life.

It is not only fathers. Some men were shaped by mothers under impossible pressure, women doing their best in circumstances that were never designed for one person to manage alone. Some men grew up in homes fractured by addiction, poverty, violence, or religious abuse that used the name of God to inflict damage He never authorized. There are men who were violated in their most vulnerable years, robbed of innocence before they even understood what innocence was.

Some men watched everything fall apart and were told, explicitly or implicitly, that they needed to be strong, that they needed to hold it together, that tears were weakness, and that need was shameful. So, they became strong the only way they knew how. They shut everything down. They closed every door that led inward. They built walls and called it character, and they walked into adulthood as functional human beings with devastated interiors.

Here is where it gets even more layered, and when most conversations about broken men stop short. That same broken home that produced emotional shutdown also produced something else in many men. It produced a distorted understanding of women, sex, and what real intimacy is supposed to be.

When a boy grows up watching his father move from woman to woman, hearing uncles brag about conquests, and viewing images that reduced women to objects before he ever had a meaningful conversation with one, he does not develop a healthy understanding of intimacy. He develops an appetite driven by pain, by the need for power, validation, and the temporary relief of something he cannot name.

Nobody ever explained to him the difference between desire and discipline. Nobody modeled what honoring a woman looked like. Nobody told him that sexual discipline is not weakness but one of the clearest marks of a man who has genuine authority over his own life.

So, he grows up carrying that distortion into every relationship. He makes choices driven not by character but by craving, not by conviction but by the hollow ache of a boy who never felt chosen, never felt affirmed, never felt like enough. And those choices cost him. They cost him his marriage, his children's trust, his reputation, his career, and sometimes his very sense of self.

The man sitting in the wreckage of a life unraveled by sexual brokenness is rarely a man who set out to destroy everything he loved. More often, he is a man who never dealt with what was broken inside him before it began affecting everything around him. The wound came first. The behavior was always just the wound looking for somewhere to go. And the crack that produced it was there long before he was old enough to understand what a crack was.

God saw every moment of it. Every single one. Psalm 139 tells us that God was present in our formation, that He knit us together in our mother's womb, that every day of our lives was written in His book before a single one of them came to pass. That means there was no season of your story, no matter how dark, no matter how damaging, that God was not fully aware of and fully present in.

He was not absent when that wound entered your life. He was not asleep when that man failed you, or that home broke apart, or that thing happened that you have never told anyone. He was there. And more than being there, He was already weaving the threads of your redemption into the very fabric of what looked like your destruction.

That truth does not erase the pain. It does not minimize what was done or what was lost. What it does is reframe the entire story. It takes the narrative out of the hands of your past and places it back into the hands of a sovereign God who specializes in building destinies out of damaged beginnings.

Joseph was thrown into a pit by his own brothers. Moses was hidden in a basket on a river. David was so overlooked by his own father that he was not even called in from the field when the prophet came to anoint a king. The pattern runs consistently through the lives of the men God used most powerfully. Their beginnings were marked by rejection, loss, displacement, and pain. God did not use them despite those beginnings. He used what they produced: resilience, hunger, and absolute dependence on Him that comfort never could have cultivated. The crack in their early lives was not an accident of history. It was the very place God was already preparing to fill with gold.

There is something that grows in a man who has had to fight for everything that never grows in a man who has had everything handed to him. There is a depth of compassion in a man who has known real suffering that a man untouched by hardship simply does not possess. There is a kind of authority in a healed man's voice that only comes from having walked through something and come out the other side with his faith in God intact.

None of that is possible without breaking. None of it develops in the absence of pressure. The very wounds you have been most ashamed of are often the exact places where your most profound gifts are buried, waiting to be excavated by the grace of God and placed in service of purposes larger than your pain.

The crack is not your disqualification. The crack is your qualification once God gets His hands on it and fills it with what only He can provide. The generational wound does not heal by being ignored. It does not resolve itself simply because time passes or because a man decides he will be different from the men who came before him.

Good intentions are not enough to break a generational cycle. Determination alone is not enough.

I have watched men swear they would never become their fathers, only to see those same patterns surface in their own homes, marriages, and relationships with their children. Not because they were weak men but because unaddressed wounds have a gravity of their own. They pull. They repeat. They reproduce.

Until someone makes the decision not just to behave differently but to be genuinely transformed from the inside out by the power of a God who breaks cycles the way He parts seas, completely, suddenly, and permanently.

That transformation begins with honesty. Not the managed kind. Not the carefully edited confession designed to release just enough pressure while protecting the image. The raw, unfiltered kind. The kind that happens between a man and God in a moment when the performance finally costs more than it is worth and something in him surrenders.

That is the moment the Potter has been waiting for. Not because God needs your breakdown to begin His work, but because you need it. You need the moment when you stop pretending the vessel is fine and allow the One who made it to pick up every broken piece and begin the slow, intentional, golden work of putting it back together in a way that makes the repair more beautiful than the original ever was.

The crack was there before you had a name for it. It was there in the home you grew up in, in the silence of the man who should have spoken, in the absence of the affirmation that should have come, and in the distortions that formed before you were old enough to question them. You did not choose any of that. You did not ask to begin the way you began.

I want you to understand something that I have come to know with absolute certainty through both Scripture and personal experience. The crack that was there before you had a name for it was also seen by a God who had a plan for it before you took your first breath. He saw it. He allowed it. And He has been preparing the gold for it longer than you have been carrying the wound. You did not choose where you started. But by the grace of God, you have a voice in where you finish.

Chapter 2

STRONG MEN DON'T CRY

(THE LIE THAT'S KILLING US)

There is a sentence that has done more damage to the interior life of men than almost any other combination of words ever spoken. It gets delivered in different ways depending on the household, culture, and generation. Sometimes it comes directly. Sometimes it comes through a look, a dismissal, or a laugh at the wrong moment.

Every man who has ever heard it knows exactly what it felt like the first time it landed. It told him that what he was feeling was unacceptable. That the tears forming in his eyes were a sign of weakness. That whatever was happening inside him needed to be shut down immediately if he had any intention of being respected, taken seriously, or considered a real man. It told him, in no uncertain terms, to be quiet about his pain. And so he was. And so he has been. And the silence has been killing him ever since.

I want to say something directly to every man carrying that sentence around like a law. What you were told was wrong. Not partially wrong. Not wrong in certain contexts but right in others. Completely, fundamentally, and destructively wrong. And the crack it produced in you, the crack of a man who learned to feel everything and express nothing, who learned to perform composure while falling apart internally, is one of the most common and costly fractures I encounter in the lives of men sitting in the wreckage of things they never intended to destroy.

The lie got in early. It shaped everything. And until a man names it for what it always was, it will continue shaping everything, quietly and invisibly, from the inside out.

The myth of the unbreakable man did not originate in Scripture. It did not come from the heart of God. It was constructed by a world that needed men to be useful, productive, soldiers, laborers, and providers, and found it inconvenient when those men had interior lives that required attention. Somewhere along the way, that cultural demand became a personal identity, and men began to believe that their value was directly tied to their ability to feel nothing, need nothing, and endure everything without complaint.

They stopped being human beings with interior lives and became machines expected to run indefinitely without maintenance, rest, or the basic acknowledgment that something inside them was breaking down. And like any machine that is never maintained, they eventually broke down in the worst possible places at the worst possible times: in their marriages, in their parenting, in their bodies, in their minds, and in their relationship with God.

What this produces in a man over time is not strength. It is a very convincing performance of strength wrapped around a core of quiet devastation. You can see it if you know what to look for. It is the man who responds to every hard question with a deflection and a joke. It is the man who stays busy enough that stillness never catches him because stillness means feeling, and feeling means confronting what he has spent years running from. It is the man who drinks a little too much a little too often, not because he enjoys it but because it is the only way he has found to turn down the volume on what is happening inside him. It is the man who has not cried in twenty years and considers that an achievement, not understanding that what he is describing is not composure but a kind of emotional death that is slowly spreading to every living thing around him.

The performance looks strong from the outside. From the inside, it is a man slowly suffocating behind the very walls he built to protect himself. And those walls, as thick and practiced as they have become, are just another form of crack, a fracture between who a man actually is and who he has been performing to be for so long that he can no longer tell the difference.

The cruelest part of this lie is how early it takes root. A boy falls and skins his knee, and before the blood has even finished surfacing, someone is already telling him to stop crying.

A teenage boy loses something that mattered deeply to him, and the men around him tell him to shake it off, to man up, to get over it. A young man sits with grief that would break anyone and is handed stoicism as the only appropriate response. By the time he reaches adulthood, he has been thoroughly trained to suppress his emotional life that he genuinely does not know what he feels anymore. He has lost access to himself. And a man who has lost access to himself cannot truly be present for his wife, cannot genuinely connect with his children, and cannot build authentic relationships with anyone because you cannot give to others what you have buried so deeply inside yourself that you can no longer find it. Now, add to that interior silence the pressure this specific generation of men is carrying in ways no previous generation has navigated in quite the same combination.

The landscape between men and women has shifted dramatically and, in many ways, rightfully so. Women are educated, accomplished, financially independent, and increasingly clear about what they will and will not accept. But something has happened alongside that progress that is not discussed honestly enough in the spaces where men gather.

A generation of men already struggling with identity and purpose is now receiving a cultural message, delivered loudly and repeatedly, that they are unnecessary. That they do not bring enough to the table. That unless they meet a specific financial threshold, unless they have the right income, the right portfolio, and the right résumé, they are not qualified to pursue love, family, or partnership.

I want to address this honestly because I believe it is cracking young men in a way that is going largely unacknowledged. A man who already does not know his worth, who was raised without affirmation, who has spent his adult life trying to earn a place at the table through performance, does not hear that cultural message as a challenge to rise higher.

He hears it as confirmation of his deepest fear. That he is fundamentally not enough. That there is no version of himself that will ever clear the bar.

When a man reaches that conclusion, one of two things happens. He exhausts himself chasing a standard that keeps moving, building his entire identity around financial achievement in a desperate attempt to qualify himself for love. Or, he withdraws entirely, concluding that the game is designed for him to lose and that the most self-protective response is to stop playing.

Neither response is healing. Both are the predictable result of a man who was never given an identity rooted in something more permanent than his performance or paycheck. Both are simply the crack getting wider under the weight of a pressure it was never designed to bear.

God never assigned a man's worth to his income. He never designed a man's purpose to be validated by his economic output or by his ability to meet the financial expectations of a culture that was never qualified to define him. Before Adam built anything, before he earned anything, before he proved anything, God looked at him and said, "It is not good for man to be alone."

The need for companionship and the value of a man's existence were established before any achievement entered the equation. The lie that a man must earn his place in a relationship, that he must reach a certain level before he is worthy of love, is a distortion of God's design that is damaging both men and women simultaneously. It is pushing men toward isolation and compulsive performance, and it is pushing women toward a self-sufficiency that can feel like empowerment but often produces a profound loneliness that accomplishment alone was not designed to fill. God's design has always been interdependence. Two people, each carrying the image of God, each incomplete without the other, coming together not because one needs to be rescued by the other but because what they build together reflects something about God that neither reflects alone.

But men are not having that conversation. They are sitting with all of it: the pressure to perform, the fear of inadequacy, the shifting expectations, and the loneliness of never being asked how they are really doing. And they are saying nothing. Because the sentence got delivered early and often enough that silence became the only language available to them when things got hard.

Somewhere between boyhood and manhood, they received the message that their inner world was a liability, and they have been managing that liability ever since by pretending it does not exist. And every year that passes without the silence being broken, the crack grows a little wider, a little deeper, and a little more resistant to the gold that has been waiting all along to fill it. Surely that prevents God from reaching it, and a wound that cannot be reached cannot be filled. It can only deepen.

I have watched men carry wounds for decades that could have been addressed in a single honest moment with God, simply because they were never willing to open the crack wide enough for the gold to enter. The performance kept them functional. But it also kept them fractured. And there is a difference between a man who is functioning and a whole man, a difference that becomes more visible and more costly with every passing year.

What God is asking of a man is not that he becomes emotionally indulgent, or that he processes every feeling publicly, or that he abandons the genuine strength that has carried him through hard seasons. What God is asking is that a man stops lying to himself about what is happening inside him. That he stops performing a wholeness he does not possess. That he brings the crack into the open, into the presence of a God who is not surprised by it, not repelled by it, and not waiting to use it as evidence against the man who carries it. He is waiting to fill it. He has always been waiting to fill it. And the filling cannot begin until the concealment ends. That is not weakness. That has always been the bravest thing a man can do.

Chapter 3

THE WEIGHT OF WHAT YOU'RE CARRYING

There is a particular kind of tired that has nothing to do with sleep. It is not the exhaustion that comes from a long week of hard work or a season of pushing through difficult circumstances. It is deeper than that and less visible than that, and most men living inside it could not fully explain it to you even if they wanted to.

It is the tiredness of a man who has been carrying something heavy for so long that he has forgotten what it feels like to walk without the weight. He has adjusted his entire posture around it. He has restructured his life to accommodate it. He has become so accustomed to the burden that its presence feels normal and its absence feels unimaginable.

And so he keeps carrying. He keeps moving. He keeps performing. And the weight keeps accumulating, quietly and invisibly, until one day something gives way and the people around him are shocked because they never saw it coming, even though it had been building for years right in front of them.

I want to talk about what men are actually carrying, not in generalities but specifically, because one of the ways the enemy keeps a man trapped beneath his weight is by convincing him that what he carries is too unique, too shameful, or too far gone ever to be brought into the light. He keeps it nameless because nameless things feel more permanent. They feel more defined. They feel more isolated.

A man who cannot name what he is carrying cannot ask for help with it, and a man who cannot ask for help is a man who will carry it until it destroys something in him that was never meant to be destroyed. So, let me name some things. Not to expose anyone but to create the kind of honest environment where a man can finally look at what is in his hands, call it what it is, and begin to understand that the weight he has been managing alone was never meant to be carried that way.

Shame is perhaps the heaviest thing a man carries, and it is the one he is least likely to name. There is a difference between guilt and shame that matters enormously for a man trying to understand what is happening inside him. Guilt says, "I did something wrong." Shame says, "I am doing something wrong." Guilt points to a behavior. Shame points to an identity.

Once shame takes root in a man's interior life, it does not stay contained in the area it originated. It spreads. It colors the way he sees himself in every room he enters, every relationship he attempts, and every opportunity that presents itself. It whispers that he is a fraud, that if people knew the truth about him, they would leave, and that whatever good he manages to produce is merely borrowed time before the real version of him is exposed.

Shame is the reason men perform rather than connect. It is the reason a man can be surrounded by people who love him and still feel completely alone. It is the reason so many men sabotage the very things they worked hardest to build, because something deep inside has already decided they do not deserve to keep them. What shame does to a crack is make it wider.

Every time a man rehearses the verdict that shame has spoken over him, every time he agrees with the voice that says he is too far gone, too damaged, or too much of a contradiction to be genuinely used by God, that crack deepens. And a crack that keeps deepening is a crack that demands more energy to conceal, more performance to cover, and more distance to maintain between the man and anyone who might get close enough to see what is actually there.

The gold cannot fill what shame keeps reopening. Which is why the work of healing for a man always has to begin at the level of identity before it can meaningfully address behavior. A man who believes he is fundamentally defective will unconsciously work to prove that belief true, no matter how many times he resolves to do differently.

Behind the shame, in most men, is a secret. Sometimes it is one secret. Sometimes it is a collection of them, a private archive of things done and things experienced that he has never shown to another living soul. These secrets take many forms, and I want to address them without flinching because flinching is what has kept too many of us in bondage to things that the grace of God already paid for in full.

Men are carrying the weight of sexual sin that began in adolescence and never stopped. Patterns of behavior that have become compulsive, that have survived multiple attempts to quit, that have outlasted promises made to God, to themselves, and to the women they love.

They wake up every morning with the genuine intention of being different and find themselves in the same place by nightfall, hating themselves more deeply with each cycle, convinced that they are beyond the reach of the change they sincerely desire. I want to speak directly to that man because I understand the particular devastation of that cycle, the way it compounds shame with every repetition until you feel so far removed from the person you want to be that the distance itself becomes a reason to stop trying.

The crack that sexual sin carves into a man is deep and specific, and it touches his sense of identity, his relationship with God, his capacity for genuine intimacy, and his ability to lead with any sense of moral authority in his home and community. It does not stay in one area. It bleeds into everything.

It rarely begins with sex. It begins with pain. It begins with the boy who was exposed too early, who learned that his body could access something that temporarily quieted the noise inside him, and who never received the intervention that could have redirected that hunger toward wholeness. It begins with the man who never learned what genuine intimacy looks like, who confused conquest with connection, and who reached for something physical every time something emotional became too heavy to carry alone.

The behavior is real, its consequences are real, and they should not be minimized. Marriages are ending because of this. Children are raised in divided homes. Careers built over decades are collapsing. Ministries are imploding.

Reputations are being dismantled publicly in ways that follow a man for the rest of his life. But the response to those consequences cannot be condemnation alone, because condemnation without redemption leaves a man with nowhere to go except deeper into the shame that was driving the behavior in the first place. And deeper shame means a wider crack, which means a man moving farther from the gold rather than closer to it.

There are men carrying addiction in forms that reach beyond what most people picture when they hear the word. Some are addicted to substances that began as a way to manage pain and became a need that now manages them. Some are addicted to work, using productivity as an anesthetic for an interior wound that productivity was never designed to treat. Some are addicted to approval, building entire public identities around the validation of others because the validation they needed in childhood never occurred. Some are addicted to control, micromanaging every environment around them because the world they grew up in was so chaotic and unpredictable that control became the only form of safety they knew how to construct.

The substance or behavior changes, but the function remains the same. Something inside hurts too much to be left alone, and the addiction is simply what a man reached for when he needed the pain to stop. Every addiction is a crack with something temporary poured into it, something that numbs for a moment but never fills, something that must be reapplied with increasing frequency because it addresses the symptom while leaving the wound completely untouched.

Many men are living with the aftermath of things that happened to them, situations they did not choose, and circumstances they did not deserve. They were abused physically, sexually, emotionally, by people who should have been their protectors.

This is a reality that rarely gets discussed in spaces where men gather because the shame attached to male victimization runs so deep that most men would rather carry the wound silently for the rest of their lives than risk being seen as someone to whom that happened.

And so they carry it into their sexuality, where it often produces confusion, compulsion, or complete shutdown. They carry it into their relationships, where it manifests as hypervigilance, distrust, or an anger that seems disproportionate to the moments that trigger it. They carry it into their parenting, terrified of repeating what was done to them or overcompensating in ways that create entirely different problems.

The wound shapes everything, even when it remains unnamed. The crack it produced, wide and deep and hidden beneath layers of performance and self-protection, is one of the places where God most wants to pour His gold, because the depth of the fracture is matched exactly by the depth of the restoration He has prepared for it.

Isaiah 53:4 tells us that Jesus Himself was acquainted with grief, that He carried our sorrows. That is not poetic language designed merely to produce a feeling. It is a theological declaration that the God who made you has personal knowledge of the weight you are carrying. He is not observing your burden from a comfortable distance.

He entered into human suffering completely enough to carry it in His own body.

This means that when a man brings his weight to God, he is not presenting it to someone who cannot relate. He is bringing it to the only One who ever fully understood what it costs a man to carry what should never be carried alone. And more than understanding it, He absorbed it. He took it into Himself so that the weight a man carries would never have to become his permanent address.

Let me say something to the man who has been carrying his weight for so long that he has stopped believing it is possible to put it down. The weight was never designed to be permanent. It was designed to be surrendered.

Not managed better. Not redistributed more efficiently. Not carried with more sophisticated coping mechanisms. Surrendered completely. Placed in the hands of a God who is not overwhelmed by its size, complexity, or history, who looks at everything in that archive of secrets and shame and does not recoil, who sees the full inventory of what a man has been carrying and responds not with condemnation but with an invitation. Matthew 11:28 does not say, "Come to me, all who have it together." It says, "Come to me, all who are weary and burdened, and I will give you rest."

The invitation was never extended to the composed. It was always extended to the carrying. The crack that all this weight has produced in a man is not a small crack. In most men, it is a system of fractures, interconnected and deep, running through his identity, relationships, sexuality, faith, and sense of purpose.

I want you to understand something about what the Kintsugi artist does with a vessel that carries fractures like that. He does not look at the extent of the damage and conclude that the piece is too far gone. The more extensive the fracture, the more gold is required to fill it. And the more gold that is required, the more breathtaking the finished piece becomes.

The most celebrated Kintsugi pieces are not the ones that were barely damaged. They are the ones that looked most beyond repair, that were gathered fragment by fragment from the floor and brought back to wholeness by hands that never lost confidence in what the finished piece was going to become.

You are not too broken. You may be exactly broken enough for the kind of repair that leaves people unable to explain what they are looking at, apart from the grace of God.

There is a moment that changes a man's life, and it rarely happens on a stage or in a crowd. It happens alone, in a quiet place, when he finally stops negotiating with God about which parts of himself he is willing to surrender. When he stops bringing the edited version and brings the real one instead. When the performance finally exhausts itself and something underneath it, something that has been waiting a very long time, finally speaks the truth out loud. That moment is not the end of anything. It is the beginning of everything the gold was always meant to fill.

Chapter 4

WHEN GOD DOES THE BREAKING

A theology that has been preached so frequently and so enthusiastically in certain circles has become the default expectation of an entire generation of believers. It promises that faith produces comfort, that obedience guarantees protection, and that a life surrendered to God is a life insulated from catastrophic loss. It fills arenas, moves crowds, and sells millions of books, and it is, at its core, a half-truth dressed up as the full gospel.

While God is absolutely a God of blessing, provision, and supernatural intervention on behalf of His people, He is also something this comfortable theology has almost no category for. He is a God who sometimes does the breaking Himself. And for the man who has built his faith on the promise of uninterrupted blessing, the moment that breaking arrives can feel like the end of everything he thought he believed.

I want to be honest with you about something that most Christian books will not say directly. Sometimes the breaking in your life did not come from the enemy. Sometimes it did not come from your own poor choices. Sometimes it did not come from the fallen world operating according to its broken nature.

Sometimes it came from God. Not from a God who stopped loving you. Not from a God who grew impatient with your progress and decided to press you back into alignment through pain. But from a God who loved you completely and was so committed to the fullness of what He placed inside you that He allowed, and sometimes orchestrated, the very circumstances that dismantled the version of your life that was too small for the purpose He had always intended. The breaking was not the absence of His love. It was one of its most specific and costly expressions.

That truth is hard to receive when you are sitting in the rubble. I know that from personal experience. But I also know that a man who never receives it will spend the rest of his life misinterpreting the most important chapters of his story, calling sovereign preparation random suffering, calling divine disruption divine abandonment, and carrying an offense against God through seasons that were actually His most intentional and purposeful work in a man's life.

The Potter does not break the vessel carelessly. He breaks it with a finished picture already in mind, with the gold already prepared, and with hands that have never once acted without intention toward the piece they are holding.

Job was not a sinful man living in rebellion when everything he had was taken. Scripture is explicit on this point. He was blameless and upright, who feared God and turned away from evil. He was not being disciplined. He was not reaping a harvest of bad decisions. He was a righteous man who lost his children, his wealth, his health, and nearly his sanity—not because he had done something wrong but because God, in His sovereignty, allowed an assault that no human logic can fully explain.

What makes Job's story so important for a man sitting in the middle of his own devastation is not that it ends with restoration, though it does. It is that in the middle of the devastation, before the restoration came, before any explanation was offered, Job did not abandon God. He wrestled with Him. He cried out to Him. He said things that made his friends deeply uncomfortable and that God later described as more honest than anything the friends had said. God met him in that honest, agonizing, unresolved place before He ever answered a single question.

That is the God who is present in your breaking. Not on the other side of it, waiting for you to get through it on your own. Present inside it, closer than the pain itself, working in the fracture with a precision and intentionality that the breaking itself conceals from the man experiencing it.

Joseph spent thirteen years in circumstances that, by any reasonable measure, looked like the complete unraveling of a promise God Himself had given. Thirteen years from the pit to the prison to the forgotten corner of Pharaoh's dungeon. Thirteen years of watching the dream God placed inside him appear to move farther away with every passing season rather than closer.

There is no record in Scripture that God spoke to Joseph during those thirteen years. No vision, no angelic visitation, no burning bush moment to reassure him that everything was on track. Just silence, suffering, and the slow grinding work of a process that would have broken a lesser man entirely. But what those thirteen years were producing in Joseph could not have been produced any other way. The character required to govern a nation, to steward unprecedented power without being corrupted by it, to forgive the brothers who sold him when he had every earthly reason to destroy them, that character was being forged in the darkness of a dungeon where no one was watching, and God appeared to be absent.

God was not absent. He was working in the crack. He was filling every fracture that the pit and prison produced with the gold of a character so refined and tested that when the moment of Joseph's appointment finally arrived, the man who stepped into it was exactly the man the moment required. The years that looked like waste were not waste. They were the most intensive preparation God ever ran a man through, and the gold that filled every crack of those thirteen years became the most visible and enduring thing about Joseph's legacy.

I have watched men in my own experience go through seasons that looked, from the outside, like pure devastation. Seasons where everything they had built came down. Where the thing they loved most was taken. Where the calling they were most certain about seemed to evaporate without explanation.

I have watched some of those men make the decision that Job made, the decision to stay in the presence of God, even when God felt absent, to keep bringing the broken pieces to the Potter, even when the Potter seemed to be the one doing the breaking. Without exception, every man who made that decision eventually arrived at a place where he could see, with a clarity that only comes from the other side of the process, that God had not wasted a single moment of the suffering. Every crack had been intentional. Every fracture had been filled with something that the comfortable seasons never could have produced.

Isaiah 45:7 contains one of the most jarring statements God makes about Himself in all of Scripture. He declares that He forms light and creates darkness, that He makes peace and creates calamity. Not that He permits it reluctantly from a distance. Not that He allows it when evil forces press their advantage beyond what He can contain.

He takes ownership of it. He claims authorship over the difficult chapters in a way that dismantles the comfortable theology that would prefer a God who is only ever behind the blessings and never behind the breaking.

The God of Scripture is not that manageable. He is not that domesticated. He is sovereign over the full spectrum of human experience, and His sovereignty does not become uncomfortable when life gets hard. It remains the same sovereignty that split the Red Sea, raised the dead, and brought order out of chaos in the opening verses of creation.

The breaking was not a surprise to Him. The loss was not a failure of divine attention. The season that dismantled everything you had built was not evidence that God had taken His hand off your life. It was, as painful as this is to receive, evidence that He had not. A God who was truly absent would have left you alone in your comfortable insufficiency.

The breaking is the fingerprint of a God who loves you too much to let you remain in a version of your life that was too small for the purpose He assigned you before you were born. The crack He allowed was not punishment. It was preparation. And the preparation was always, from the very beginning, oriented toward the gold.

Romans 8:28, one of the most quoted verses in Christian culture, is also one of the most superficially applied.

Men hear that all things work together for good and interpret it as a promise that everything will eventually feel good, that every painful chapter will be followed quickly by a comfortable one that makes the pain seem worthwhile in retrospect. But that is not what the verse is saying. It is saying that God, in His active sovereignty, takes every single element of a man's story, including the chapters that should not have happened, including the wounds that came from other people's sin, including the consequences of a man's own failures, and works them together toward a purpose that is good in the deepest and most eternal sense of the word.

Not comfortable necessarily. Not painless certainly. But purposeful absolutely.

Oriented toward something that matters in a way that transcends the temporary experience of suffering and produces in a man something far more valuable than the comfort he lost when the breaking began.

The man in the middle of his breaking cannot always see this. That is not a failure of faith. That is the honest limitation of a human being who can only see what is directly in front of him. Faith is not the ability to see what God is doing. Faith is the decision to trust that He is doing something even when you cannot see it. It is the choice made in the dark to believe that the silence is not absence, that the pressure is not punishment, and that the God who allowed this season into your story has not lost the pen and has not lost sight of the finished piece He is working toward.

Jeremiah 18 tells us that when the vessel became marred in the potter's hands, the potter reworked it into another vessel as it seemed good to the potter to do. The potter did not discard the marred clay. He did not call it a failure and reach for fresh material. He took the same clay, clay that had already been worked and shaped and had been through the wheel before, and reworked it according to the good he had always intended for it.

Nothing was discarded. Not the previous shaping. Not the fracture. Not the damage. In the potter's hands, everything that already happened to the clay became material for what the potter was building next. The marring was not the end of the story. It was the moment the potter's most intentional work began. That is God's economy with a broken man. He does not discard the history; He incorporates it.

The years of the breaking become the substance of the testimony. The cracks become channels through which the gold flows most deeply and most permanently. The finished piece, the man who has been through the breaking and the reworking and the filling, carries something a that man who was never broken simply does not possess. He carries the gold. Visible. Permanent. Impossible to explain apart from the hands that placed it there and the breaking that made room for it.

The question a man must settle in the middle of his breaking is not why. It is a reasonable question, but it is rarely the one God answers on demand. Waiting for the answer to why before being willing to trust is a posture that leaves a man stranded indefinitely in the middle of the very process that was designed to move him forward into something greater. What God is asking is simpler and harder at the same time. He is not asking for understanding. He is not asking for approval. He is asking whether, in the absence of explanation, in the presence of pain that does not yet have a name, a man is willing to trust the hands that are holding the broken pieces and that have never once dropped what they intended to restore.

The Potter has never abandoned a piece He intended to repair. Not once in all of Scripture. Not once in human history. Not in the life of a single man who surrendered the breaking to the One who allowed it and who had the gold ready before the first crack appeared. He is not about to start with yours.

Chapter 5

THE WOUNDS THAT SHAPED YOU

There is a difference between a wound that shapes you and a wound that controls you, and most men have never stopped long enough to figure out which one they are living with. They know something happened. They know it left a mark. They can feel its effect in the way they react to certain situations, in the patterns that keep repeating in their relationships, and in the walls that rise without warning when someone gets too close to a particular place inside them. But because they have never named it, never traced it back to its origin, never stood in front of it long enough to see it clearly, it continues to operate from the shadows of their lives, shaping decisions, sabotaging relationships, and quietly determining the ceiling of everything they attempt to build.

Every man has a wound with a name on it. Not a general wound, not a vague sense that life has been hard, but a specific injury that arrived at a specific moment and changed something fundamental about the way he saw himself and the world around him. For some men, it is the wound of rejection, delivered by a father who never showed up, a woman who left, a community that excluded them, or a God who seemed silent at the moment His presence was needed most.

For some men, it is the wound of failure, a moment or season when everything they attempted collapsed, and the collapse became the lens through which they evaluated every subsequent risk. For some men, it is the wound of betrayal, the particular devastation that comes when someone who was supposed to be safe proves to be anything but. For some men, it is a wound that arrived without the participation of anyone else at all, a loss, a diagnosis, a circumstance that simply happened and took something irreplaceable with it when it left.

I have carried wounds from more than one of those categories. What I know from personal experience, not just from Scripture or from the lives of men I have walked alongside, is that a wound left unaddressed does not stay the size it was when it arrived. It grows. It becomes more influential with time, not less, because the longer a man goes without bringing it to God, the more of his life gets organized around protecting it.

He makes decisions based on a wound without realizing it. He avoids certain rooms, certain conversations, and certain levels of intimacy, not because those things are genuinely dangerous but because they are near the wound, and the wound has taught him that anything close enough to touch it is a threat. He builds an entire architecture of avoidance around something he has never once looked at directly. That architecture keeps expanding to keep pace with the wound as it grows, consuming more of the man's energy and more of the life God intended him to inhabit freely.

Whatever the wound, it did not stay contained to the moment it arrived. Wounds never do. They migrate. They embed themselves into the operating system of a man's interior life and begin to influence everything that runs through it.

The man who was abandoned develops a wound that follows him into every relationship, making him desperate for reassurance or preemptively distant, because some part of him has already decided that closeness is only the precondition for loss. The man who was shamed develops a wound that makes him either a relentless overachiever, constantly trying to earn his way out of the verdict that was spoken over him, or a man who never fully commits to anything because commitment means being seen, and being seen means being found out.

The wound becomes the architect. The man living inside the structure it built has often forgotten that there was ever any other way to live, that the structure was constructed around the wound and not around him, and that the God who made him never intended for him to spend his life inside it. This is where the story of a man's identity becomes the most important conversation he can have with himself and with God.

Identity is not what happened to you. Identity is not the sum of your wounds, failures, worst moments, or the worst things that were said about you by people who did not have the authority to define you in the first place. Identity, for a man who belongs to God, is what God declared about you before any of those things happened, and what He has continued to declare about you despite all of them.

The world will always attempt to hand a man his identity through the events of his life. God hands a man his identity through the declaration of His Word. And those two sources are in constant competition for the authority to determine how a man sees himself when he looks in the mirror and how he moves through the world when nobody is watching.

The crack that a wound produces is real. I will not minimize that by rushing too quickly to the redemptive side of the story. The crack is real. It has depth. It has history. It has produced real consequences in a man's life and in the lives of the people who love him.

Here is what I have come to know with absolute certainty through both Scripture and watching God work in the lives of broken men, including my own. The crack is not the final statement about who a man is. The gold that God fills it with is the final statement. And the gold does not erase the crack. It inhabits it. It makes the fracture permanently visible in a way that announces to everyone who sees it not what was broken, but what was restored, and more importantly, by whose hands the restoration was accomplished and at what cost that gold was prepared.

David understood the competition between wound and identity in a deeply personal way. The same man who slew Goliath with a stone was the man his own father did not think worth calling in from the field when the prophet came to anoint a king. Jesse presented every other son before Samuel had to specifically ask whether there were any remaining. David was not even in the room.

His own father's assessment of him was so low that he did not factor into consideration at all. That is a wound with a very specific shape. The wound of being invisible to the man whose approval mattered most.

However, God said something entirely different about David than his father's absence said. God looked past everything that impressed everyone else and saw the heart of a man He had already chosen and already prepared gold for. The wound of being overlooked did not disqualify David from his destiny. But it also did not disappear quietly.

It showed up later in his life in the hunger for validation that contributed to some of his most costly decisions. The wound shaped him. The question was always whether he would allow God to transform what it had produced in him or whether he would allow it to continue operating from the shadows unchecked, widening the crack instead of surrendering it to be filled.

Some men have allowed their wounds to become their entire personality. The pain became so central to their experience that they began to organize their lives around it, protecting it, ensuring it was never touched again. They constructed identities around being the man to whom something terrible happened, not because victimhood is comfortable, but because it is at least familiar, and familiarity, even when it's painful, feels safer than the unknown territory of genuine healing.

Other men went in the opposite direction and allowed their wounds to become fuel for overcorrection, becoming so driven, so controlled, so determined never to be vulnerable again that they achieved remarkable things externally while becoming increasingly hollow internally. Neither response is healing. Both are sophisticated forms of avoidance dressed in the clothing of coping. And avoidance, no matter how productive it looks from the outside, is still just a man running from a crack he has never been willing to surrender to the One who has the gold to fill it.

2 Corinthians 12:9 carries one of the most counter-intuitive statements in Scripture. God tells Paul directly that His strength is made perfect in weakness and His grace is sufficient for every place where Paul's own capacity runs out. Paul's response to that word is extraordinary. He says he will boast in his weaknesses, that he will take pleasure in his infirmities, because he has discovered that the places where he is weakest are the very places where the power of God rests most visibly upon him.

That is not a man who learned to ignore his wounds. That is a man who learned to bring them to God so consistently and so honestly that they were transformed from liabilities into access points for divine power. The wound did not disappear. It was redeemed. The crack did not close. It was filled. And the filling made the wound more useful than wholeness ever could have been, because the gold that inhabited the crack became the most powerful and undeniable evidence of God's presence and grace in Paul's life and in everything he built.

This is the work God is inviting every broken man into. Not the erasure of what happened. Not pretending that the wound was not real or did not cost what it cost. But the full and honest surrender of it to a God who can do something with it that the man himself never could.

I have seen this happen in real time in the lives of men who had carried wounds for twenty and thirty years; wounds they had decided were simply permanent features of who they were, and who discovered in a moment of genuine surrender that God was already there when the crack finally opened. Not eventually ready. Already there. Already holding the gold. Already knowing exactly where every fracture ran and exactly how much filling it would take to make the finished piece more breathtaking than anything the original wholeness could have produced.

There is a moment in every man's journey when he has to decide his wounds. He has to decide whether they are going to remain the defining story of his life or whether he is going to allow God to write a larger story around them. Whether the crack is going to be the thing people see when they look at him, or whether the gold God fills it with is going to become the most visible and powerful thing about who he is. That decision does not happen once and stay settled.

It happens repeatedly, every time the wound gets triggered, every time an old pattern tries to reassert itself, every time shame tries to reclaim the territory that grace has already purchased.

Healing is not a single moment. It is a direction. It is the daily choice to keep moving toward God with the broken pieces rather than away from Him with them, to keep surrendering what surfaces rather than reburying it, to keep trusting that the Potter knows exactly what He is doing even when the reworking is painful, and the new shape is not yet visible to the man being remade.

Genesis 50:20 is one of the most powerful declarations about redemptive purpose ever recorded. Joseph, standing before the brothers who sold him into slavery, having lived through everything that sale produced in his life, says something that no man arrives at cheaply or quickly. He tells them that what they intended for evil, God intended for good. Not that God caused the evil. Not that the evil was not real or did not hurt. But that God, in His sovereign purposefulness, took what was meant to destroy and turned it into the very mechanism of deliverance for an entire generation.

Joseph could only say that from the other side of the process. He could not have said it from the pit. He could not have said it from prison. He said it after God had done what only God can do with a wound that has been fully surrendered, after the gold had been poured in and had set, after the crack had become the most luminous thing about him rather than the most shameful.

That is where God is taking every man who is willing to bring his wounds honestly and completely to the One who already knows every detail of every one of them. Not to a place where the wound is erased, or the history is revised. But to a place where a man can look at the most painful chapters of his story and recognize in every one of them the fingerprints of a God who was present, who wasted nothing, who used everything, and who is still, even now, filling the cracks with a gold so permanent and so luminous that the wound itself becomes the most compelling evidence of His grace in a man's life.

The wound shaped you. But it does not own you. The crack is real. But so is the gold. And the God who fills one with the other has never once run out of either.

Chapter 6

BROKEN RELATIONSHIPS AND THE MEN WHO GAVE UP

There is a particular kind of grief that a man carries when a relationship he built with his own hands falls apart in front of him. It is not the clean grief of loss that arrives when something is taken without warning and the man had no part in it. It is the heavier and more complicated grief of watching something he loved, something he was supposed to protect, something he may have even prayed over, unravel in ways he could not stop or in ways he directly contributed to.

It sits differently in a man's chest than other kinds of pain. It mingles with regret and shame and the relentless internal cross examination that asks what he could have done differently, what he should have seen coming, and whether the outcome would have been different if he had been a different kind of man. And it leaves a crack unlike almost any other crack a man carries, because this one has witnesses. This one has names attached to it. This one lives in the faces of the people he loves most and could not keep.

I have sat with men in the aftermath of relational devastation that would have broken anyone. Men who watched marriages they had invested everything into dissolve. Men who picked up the phone to call a child and heard the careful politeness of a relationship that had gone cold. Men who looked across a room at the person they loved most in the world and felt a distance so established and so wide that closing it seemed more impossible than simply accepting it as the new permanent condition of their lives.

What I have observed consistently in those conversations is that the grief a man carries from broken relationships is rarely simple. It is layered with things he did and things he failed to do, with moments he cannot recover and words he cannot unsay, with the particular weight of a man who knows that the people he hurt the most were the people he loved the most, and who cannot reconcile those two realities into anything that produces peace.

Broken relationships are one of the most universal experiences of the human condition and one of the least honestly discussed realities in the lives of men. Men are not typically taught how to grieve a relationship. They are not given language for the specific devastation of a marriage that ends, a son who stops returning calls, a daughter who looks at her father with eyes that no longer hold trust, or a friendship that quietly dissolves under the weight of distance and neglect. They are simply expected to move on, to stay functional, to keep producing, and to process whatever they feel about relational loss in whatever private space they can find, which for most men means not processing it at all.

Eventually, it accumulates. It joins everything else in the archive of things carried but never addressed. And it shapes the way a man approaches subsequent relationships, often making him either more guarded or more desperate, neither of which produces the connection he was actually built for, and neither of which does anything except widen the crack that the broken relationship left behind.

Marriage is where this pain tends to be most acute. There is something about the dissolution of a marriage that strikes at the core of a man's identity in ways that other losses do not quite replicate. A man's marriage is linked to his sense of himself as a provider, a protector, a leader, and a lover. When it fails, failure does not feel contained to the relationship. It feels like an indictment of who he is as a man. Because men have been conditioned to tie their worth to their performance, a failed marriage becomes evidence in the court of his own interior that he was not enough, that he did not have what it took, that the most important assignment he was ever given was one he could not complete.

That verdict, once rendered internally, is one of the hardest things for a man to appeal, because he is simultaneously the prosecutor, the defendant, and the judge. The sentence he gives himself is almost always harsher than anything anyone else would impose, leaving a crack in his identity that he carries into every room, every opportunity, and every subsequent relationship he attempts to build.

Then, there is the distance from his children. A man can survive almost anything if he believes his children still need him, still see him, still carry some version of genuine love for him in their hearts. But the man who has watched that connection erode, who picks up the phone and hears the careful politeness of a child who has learned to manage their relationship with their father rather than genuinely inhabit it, who shows up to events and feels the invisible wall that his own failures constructed between himself and the people he loves most, that man is carrying a weight that has no clean name and no easy resolution.

It is the compound grief of lost time, lost trust, and the haunting awareness that children grow up whether their father gets himself together or not. Some seasons, once missed, cannot simply be recovered by good intentions arriving late. The crack that this distance produces is one of the deepest a man can carry because it is connected to the most fundamental assignment God ever gave him.

The men who gave up on relationships did not all give up at once. Most of them gave up incrementally, one small withdrawal at a time, one avoided conversation at a time, one unresolved conflict at a time, until the distance between themselves and the people they loved became so vast and so established that closing it felt more impossible than simply accepting it. They did not set out to become absent. They set out to protect themselves from a pain they did not know how to navigate, and absence was the only tool their unhealed interior had available.

They pulled back from their marriages when intimacy became too exposing. They pulled back from their children when emotional demands exceeded what their own unaddressed wounds could produce. They pulled back from friendships when the vulnerability required to sustain genuine connection felt too costly, given everything else they were already carrying. And each withdrawal made the next one easier until pulling back became the default posture in every relationship they encountered, and the crack of isolation became the defining feature of their interior landscape.

The crack that produces this pattern is almost always older than the relationship it eventually damaged. A man who never learned to be emotionally present did not develop that deficiency in his marriage. He brought it in with him from a home where presence was either modeled poorly or not modeled at all. A man who responds to relational pressure with shutdown or explosion did not acquire that response after the wedding. It was already in him, formed in the earliest relationships of his life and embedded in the crack of his generational inheritance.

The marriage, friendship, or parenting relationship simply became the context where the preexisting fracture finally became impossible to ignore. The tragedy is that by the time it became impossible to ignore, it had already done damage that would take years of intentional work to begin to address.

God never designed a man to live in relational isolation. The declaration in Genesis 2 that it was not good for man to be alone was not exclusively a commentary on romantic partnership. It was a statement about the fundamental nature of a man made in the image of a relational God. A man was built for genuine connection. He was designed to need people, to be known by people, to carry and be carried by the community of relationships God intended to surround his life.

The isolation broken men retreat into is not strength. It is a wound that has convinced itself it is a preference. And the longer a man lives inside that isolation, the more natural it feels, and the more foreign and threatening the alternative becomes, until he has so thoroughly sealed the crack of his relational capacity that nothing can get in, nothing can get out, and the gold has no surface left to fill.

Malachi 4:6 speaks of God turning the hearts of fathers back to their children and the hearts of children back to their fathers. That verse exists because the disconnection between fathers and children is not a modern invention. It is an ancient wound that God took seriously enough to address through His prophet and seriously enough to promise divine intervention in.

The heart of a father that has gone cold toward his children, or the heart of a child that has hardened against a father who was not there, is not beyond the reach of a God who specializes in turning things. Not fixing them from the outside with pressure and obligation, but turning them from the inside with a grace that softens what time and pain have made rigid and fills what distance has left hollow. The crack in that relationship, no matter how wide it has become and no matter how long it has been open, is not beyond the reach of gold. I have seen God fill relational fractures that looked permanent with a restoration so specific and complete that the only explanation for it was the active intervention of a God who takes cracked relationships as seriously as He takes cracked men.

Joel 2:25 contains a promise that every man carrying the grief of relational loss needs to receive personally and specifically. God declares that He will restore the years the locust has eaten. The locust in a man's relational life takes many forms. It is the years lost to emotional unavailability. The years lost to the kind of selfish self-preservation that sacrificed relationships on the altar of personal comfort. The years lost to not knowing how to be the husband, father, or friend the people in his life needed him to be.

God does not promise that the lost years will be returned as if they never happened. He promises restoration, and restoration is something more creative and more powerful than simple reversal. It is God taking what was lost and producing from the remaining time a harvest so abundant that it compensates for what the locusts consumed.

The crack does not disappear in the restoration. It gets filled with something more valuable than what was there before the damage began, and the seam where the repair was made becomes a visible testimony of what God can do with a relationship that every reasonable observer had written off.

Restoration requires a man to show up. It requires him to resist the voice that tells him it is too late, that too much has been lost, that the people he hurt have moved too far past him for the distance to ever be closed. That voice is not wisdom, and it is not realism. It is the enemy of everything God is trying to rebuild, and it speaks loudest precisely at the moments when a man is closest to doing something that could change everything.

The prodigal's father in Luke 15 did not wait for his son to arrive at the door with a polished apology and a credible plan for the future. He saw him coming from a great distance and ran. He ran before the speech was delivered. He ran before the repentance was fully articulated. He ran because the return of someone he loved was more important than the protection of his own dignity. And that posture of running toward rather than waiting in wounded pride is one of the most powerful pictures in all of Scripture of what a man who has been genuinely changed by grace looks like in the context of a broken relationship he still loves.

A man who wants his relationships restored has to become the one who moves first. Not because he was entirely wrong in every conflict. Not because the other party bears no responsibility for what broke. But because someone has to move first, and a man who has encountered the grace of God has been given both the model and the resource to be that person. He has been shown what it looks like to be pursued before he deserved it, embraced before he earned it, and restored before he had fully demonstrated that he was worth restoring. And having received that from God, he has something genuine and gold-filled to extend to the people his brokenness pushed away.

The relationship is not always fully restored this side of eternity. Some people will not receive what a changed man is offering. Some doors, once closed, do not reopen regardless of the sincerity of the knock. And a man must learn to hold that reality without allowing it to become the reason he stops trying, stops growing, or stops becoming the man that the people still in his life need him to be.

The work of becoming whole is not contingent on the response of the people who were hurt by the broken version. It is contingent on the faithfulness of a God who is committed to finishing what He started, regardless of what the relational landscape looks like in the process. Sometimes, the most powerful testimony a restored man carries is not a fully reconciled relationship but a genuinely changed man standing at a door that has not yet opened, still knocking, still believing, with gold visible in every crack that the waiting has produced.

The seam where a broken relationship was repaired is always visible. No version of restored trust looks exactly like trust that was never broken. But in the hands of God, that visible seam is not a reminder of failure. It is a testimony of what grace can accomplish when a man finally decides that the people he loves are worth the humility it costs to fight for them. The crack in the relationship does not have to be the final word on what that relationship becomes. In the right hands, with the right gold, the place where it broke can become the most luminous and enduring part of the story that the relationship tells.

I have watched God do this. I have watched Him take relationships that every human observer had written off and restore them with a completeness that left everyone who witnessed it without an explanation that did not begin and end with God. He takes cracked relationships seriously. He has not written off the marriage, the child, the friendship, or the connection that your brokenness damaged. And He is not waiting for a perfect man to begin the repair.

He is waiting for a willing one, a man who has placed his own broken pieces in the Potter's hands and who is ready to extend the same grace to the broken relationships around him that God extended to the broken man within him. The crack in the relationship does not have to be the end of the story. It can be the place where the gold goes.

And gold in the right crack changes everything about what the finished piece becomes and everything about the story it tells to everyone who sees it.

Chapter 7

THE CRISIS OF PURPOSE

(MEN WITHOUT A REASON TO RISE)

There is a kind of man nobody talks about because he does not fit the categories that get attention. He is not visibly addicted. He is not in legal trouble. He has not made headlines with a dramatic failure or public collapse.

He gets up every morning, goes through the motions of a life that looks reasonable from the outside, pays his bills when he can, shows up where he is supposed to show up, and returns home at the end of the day to sit in a silence that he has stopped trying to explain even to himself. He is not in crisis in any way that the people around him would recognize. But something in him has gone quiet in a way that terrifies him on the rare occasions he slows down enough to notice it. He has lost his reason to rise. Not his ability to get up, but his reason to.

A man without a reason is in a more dangerous place than most people around him will ever understand. The crack that purposelessness produces does not announce itself with drama. It opens slowly, quietly, and by the time anyone notices it, including the man himself, it has been widening for years.

I have sat across from that man more times than I can count. Sometimes he comes in dressed well, carrying the appearance of a life that is working. Sometimes he comes in barely holding the surface together. But underneath the presentation, the condition is the same. Something that was supposed to be burning inside him has gone out.

What I have learned from those conversations is that the extinguishing rarely happened all at once. It happened the way a fire dies when nobody tends it, gradually and quietly, one unaddressed need at a time, one deferred dream at a time, one season of silence too many, until the man sitting across from me had forgotten that the fire was ever there to begin with.

I have also learned is that a fire God lit does not go out permanently. It goes dormant. And dormant is not dead. Dormant is waiting for someone to bring it what it was always designed to burn on.

Purposelessness is one of the most devastating conditions a man can inhabit and also one of the most invisible. The man in an active crisis gets attention. People rally, intervene, express concern, and mobilize resources.

The man who has simply stopped believing that his life means anything drifts through his days in a quiet that nobody flags as an emergency, because he is still functioning, still present, still checking the boxes society uses to measure whether a man is okay. He is not okay. He is disappearing in plain sight, and the disappearance is so gradual and so unremarkable that by the time anyone notices, including the man himself, it has been happening for years.

The crack of purposelessness is one of the most deceptive fractures a man can carry because it does not bleed visibly. It simply drains, slowly and steadily, until a man finds himself standing in the middle of a life he built, feeling nothing about any of it. The roots of this crisis almost always run deeper than circumstance.

A man does not lose his sense of purpose simply because his career stalled or his plans did not materialize on schedule. Those things can trigger the crisis, but they do not create it. The crisis was already there, waiting beneath the surface, in the unresolved question of who a man is when you strip away everything he does.

When the job is gone, when the role is removed, when the title no longer applies, when the children have grown and left, when the relationship that organized his days has ended, what remains? Who is he? What is he for? What is the actual substance of his existence beyond the functions he performs and the obligations he fulfills?

Most men have never been taught to answer those questions because most men were never taught that those questions mattered. They were taught to produce. They were taught to provide. They were taught to perform. But nobody sat them down and helped them understand that beneath all the doing, there needed to be a being, a settled, rooted, and God given sense of identity and assignment that could sustain a man through every season, including the ones where the doing became impossible and the performing ran out.

When the doing becomes impossible and there is nothing underneath it, the crack that opens in a man is not a surface crack. It goes all the way down to the foundation. It reaches the place where a man's sense of his own value lives, and it asks a question that a man without a God given answer cannot survive intact. It asks what he is worth if he is not producing anything.

For a man who was never given an identity rooted in something more permanent than his output, that question has no satisfactory answer. So he either drives himself harder to resume producing, which is just the crack getting wider under increasing pressure, or he stops trying altogether, which is the crack becoming a collapse. Either way, the fracture deepens. Either way, the gold that was prepared for it cannot reach it because the man is too busy managing the crack to open it.

Proverbs 29:18 says that where there is no vision, the people perish. That word perish in the original language carries the idea of becoming unrestrained, of casting off all boundaries, of a life that has lost its form and begun to unravel at the edges. A man without vision does not simply stagnate. He unravels. He begins to make choices that a man with a clear sense of purpose and direction would never make, not because he is a bad man but because a man with no internal north star will follow whatever external force presents itself with enough appeal to fill the vacuum that vision was supposed to occupy.

He chases things that do not satisfy. He settles for things that do not challenge him. He medicates emptiness with whatever is available. Because emptiness is not circumstantial but existential, nothing he reaches for is ever quite enough to fill it.

The crack that purposelessness produces keeps widening because everything being poured into it to address the ache was never the gold it was designed to receive. This crisis is hitting the current generation of men with particular intensity because the traditional structures that once gave men a ready-made sense of purpose have either collapsed or been fundamentally renegotiated.

For generations, a man's purpose was largely defined by his role. He was the provider, protector, and patriarch. Those roles came with clear expectations, clear metrics for success, and a clear sense of where a man stood in relation to his family and his community. Whatever limitations those structures carried—and they carried real ones—they also gave men something to organize their lives around, something that told them every morning why getting up mattered. Now, those structures are in flux.

Cultural conversation about masculinity has become so charged and so contested that many men, particularly younger men, have simply opted out of it entirely, not because they do not care but because they cannot find a version of manhood they are allowed to inhabit without apology. And the exhaustion of that search eventually produces a withdrawal that looks like apathy but is actually a man whose crack has become so wide that he no longer has the structural integrity to hold a vision or sustain the weight of a purpose.

Into that already fractured landscape comes the additional pressure of a relational culture that evaluates a man's worth almost entirely based on what he earns and what he owns. A young man who was raised without a father to model purpose, who was educated in systems that did not know what to do with the specific energy of a boy becoming a man, who enters a workforce that does not always reward the kind of contribution he was built to make, and who then encounters a relational culture that tells him he is not qualified for love until he meets a financial threshold; that young man is being asked to find his reason to rise in soil that has been stripped of almost everything that reason requires to grow.

He is not lazy. He is not weak. He is a man trying to build something in conditions that were not designed for building, standing over a crack that keeps getting wider, being handed substitutes for gold and wondering why nothing he pours into the fracture ever makes it smaller.

God has never once defined a man by his economic output. When God looked at Gideon, He did not see the frightened man hiding in the winepress, threshing wheat in secret because he was too afraid to do it in the open. He saw a mighty man of valor. He called Gideon by the identity of his destiny rather than the reality of his current condition, because God has always been more interested in what He placed inside a man than in the circumstances pressing on the outside of him.

The call did not wait for Gideon to feel capable. It did not wait for his fear to be resolved or his confidence to be restored. It arrived in the middle of the hiding and declared something that the hiding had not yet disproven, because purpose, when it comes from God, is not contingent on a man's present emotional state, his current bank balance, or his standing in the eyes of a culture that was never qualified to assign his value or determine the width of his crack.

Jeremiah 29:11 declares that God knows the plans He has for a man, plans for a future and a hope, plans formed before the man ever had the capacity to contribute to or corrupt them. I want you to receive that not as a familiar verse you have heard a hundred times but as a personal declaration spoken directly into the crack of your purposelessness. God is not confused about what you are for. He is not waiting for you to get it together before He reveals the assignment. The plan exists because He made it, and it was complete before you were born. It has not expired simply because you lost sight of it for a season, or for a decade, or for what feels like most of your adult life.

The crack of purposelessness is real and deep, but it is not deeper than the gold God has prepared to fill it. The gold He fills it with is not a generic sense of meaning or a vague feeling of direction. It is a specific assignment, a particular contribution that only you are positioned to make, formed by the breaking you have been through and requiring exactly the kind of man that the breaking produced.

Ephesians 2:10 says that a man is God's workmanship, created in Christ Jesus for good works that God prepared in advance for him to walk in. The word workmanship in the original Greek is the word *poiema*, from which the English word poem is derived. You are not a random assembly of biology navigating a purposeless universe. You are a carefully composed expression of divine creativity, written with intention, structured with meaning, and released into history at a specific moment for a specific contribution that nobody else can make.

The works were prepared in advance. The path was laid before you took your first step. And the God who prepared the works is the same God who is present in the seasons when you cannot find the path, not standing at a distance watching you struggle but present inside the struggle, filling the crack of your purposelessness with a gold that will eventually make the direction not just visible but unmistakable and undeniable.

The man who has lost his reason to rise has not lost his purpose. He has lost his connection to the God who assigned it. And that connection, unlike a career or a relationship or a title or an income, is never more than a surrender away. The moment a man stops performing for God and starts being honest with God, the moment he brings the emptiness and the confusion and the extinguished fire directly to the One who lit it in the first place, is the moment the gold begins to move into the crack that purposelessness produced. Not eventually. Not after a qualifying period of demonstrated worthiness. In that moment.

God was never waiting for the man to find his purpose on his own. He was waiting for the man to stop trying to and come back to the only source from which genuine purpose, and genuine gold, has ever flowed.

You were not created to merely survive your life. You were created to mean something inside it. And the God who put that meaning in you, who prepared the gold for every crack the journey would produce, has never once forgotten what it was or lost confidence in the finished piece He is still working toward.

Chapter 8

THE MENDING

(SURRENDER AS STRENGTH)

Every man reaches a point where the performance runs out. Not gradually. All at once. After the marriage finally ends, the addiction finally costs too much, or the isolation finally becomes too heavy to justify. The gap between who he has been pretending to be and who he actually is becomes too wide to straddle any longer. In that moment, something in him faces a choice that will determine the trajectory of everything that follows.

The moment does not announce itself with ceremony or clarity. It does not arrive on a schedule or present itself with the kind of dramatic signpost that would make the decision obvious and the path forward clean. It arrives quietly, usually in the aftermath of something.

The performance finally exhausts the last reserve of energy a man had available to sustain it. It arrives in the stillness that follows collapse, in the silence that exists on the other side of every explanation a man has ever given for why he was fine, in the moment when the gap between who he has been performing to be and who he actually is becomes too wide to straddle any longer.

In that moment, something in him faces a choice that will determine the trajectory of everything that follows. He can gather what remains of his pride and begin reconstructing another version of the performance. Or he can do the thing every instinct his culture gave him tells him is weakness. He can surrender. He can open his hands. He can place every broken piece on the table and allow the One who made the vessel to finally do what only He was ever qualified to do.

I want to talk about surrender honestly because it is the most misunderstood word in the vocabulary of a broken man. Everything in a man's conditioning tells him that surrender is the moment a soldier drops his weapon and raises his hands because he has run out of options and run out of fight. It sounds like defeat. It sounds like the admission that he was not strong enough, that whatever he was attempting to hold together proved to be beyond his capacity to sustain.

For a man who has spent his entire life being evaluated on his ability to hold things together, the idea of surrender feels like the ultimate confirmation of every fear he has ever carried about his own inadequacy. So, he resists it. He negotiates around it. He finds more sophisticated ways to keep performing rather than face the one decision that could change everything.

In the resisting, the crack gets wider. In the negotiations, the fracture deepens. In the performance, the gold waits with a patience only God possesses for the moment, and the man finally opens what he has been sealing. But that understanding of surrender is itself a lie, and it is one of the most effective lies the enemy has ever deployed against the soul of a man.

The surrender God is inviting a man into is not the surrender of a defeated soldier. It is the surrender of a man who has finally become wise enough to stop fighting the wrong battle with the wrong weapons for the wrong reasons. It is not the surrender of weakness. It is the surrender of exhausted self-sufficiency to a power that was always greater and always available and always willing.

It is not giving up. It is giving up. The difference between those two things is the difference between a man who has quit and a man who has finally found the only source of strength that was ever going to be sufficient for what he was carrying and sufficient for filling what the carrying had cracked open in him.

I have been in that moment personally. The moment when the performance ran out, and there was nothing left behind it. What I discovered at that moment was not what my conditioning told me I would find.

I did not find humiliation. I did not find the confirmation of my inadequacy. I found a God who had been waiting in that exact place for longer than I had been running from it, who was not surprised by my arrival and not disappointed by my condition, who did not require me to clean myself up before He would engage with me, and who began doing something in that moment of surrender that all of my previous efforts at self-management had never been able to produce.

The crack I had been sealing against the world was the same crack He needed access to in order to pour in the gold. Surrender was simply the act of stopping the sealing and opening what I had spent years closing. That is all it was. And that is everything it was.

Romans 12:1 uses the word present. It says to present your bodies as a living sacrifice, holy and acceptable to God, which is your reasonable act of worship. The word present is deliberate and important. It is an act of volition, a conscious and intentional offering, a choice made by a man who is in full possession of his faculties and his freedom and who decides of his own will to place himself completely in the hands of God.

That is not passive. That is not the posture of a man who has given up on life or abdicated his responsibilities. That is the posture of a man who has made the most consequential and courageous decision available to a human being, the decision to stop being the primary architect of his own life and to trust the One who designed it to also direct it.

Surrender is not the end of a man's agency. It is the redirecting of it toward the only source that can make it genuinely productive and the only hands that can make something genuinely golden out of what the journey has cracked open.

David made this surrender repeatedly throughout his life, and the Psalms are the unedited record of what it looked like from the inside. It was not clean. It was not a single dramatic moment of consecration followed by a lifetime of effortless trust and uninterrupted peace. It was a man returning to God again and again with whatever the current moment held. He brought the fear and the grief and the confusion and the failure and the gratitude and the wonder without managing the presentation, laying all of it before God without negotiating about which parts were presentable and which needed to stay hidden.

Psalm 51 is perhaps the rawest example of what genuine surrender looks like in the life of a man who has failed catastrophically and knows it. David does not negotiate. He does not minimize. He does not construct a carefully worded acknowledgment designed to limit his exposure while releasing just enough pressure to feel like he has addressed the problem. He says, "Create in me a clean heart, O God, and renew a right spirit within me." He asks for the only thing that could actually address what had gone wrong, not the repair of his reputation or the management of the consequences, but the transformation of his interior. That is a man who has stopped fighting for control of the surface and has surrendered access to the depth where the crack actually runs and where the gold actually needs to go.

The Kintsugi artist cannot repair a vessel that is still being held tightly in resistant hands. The repair requires the piece to be placed on the work surface, to be still, to be fully available to the artist's hands in a way that resistance makes impossible. A man who is still gripping his broken pieces, still trying to arrange them himself into something that resembles wholeness, still insisting that he can figure out the repair if he is just given enough time and space and the right circumstances, is a man preventing the very repair he most desperately needs. The crack cannot be filled while the hands that should be open are closed around it.

Surrender is simply the act of opening the hands. Of placing the pieces on the table. Of saying to the God who made the vessel in the first place: I cannot fix this. I have tried everything I know how to try, and I am done pretending that another attempt at self-management is going to produce what only You have ever been equipped to produce. That moment is not the moment of a man's defeat. It is the moment the Artist picks up the gold, and the repair that was always prepared finally begins.

The practical reality of surrender for a man sitting in the middle of his brokenness is that it rarely feels powerful when it happens. It feels like a loss. It feels like the admission he spent years trying to avoid. It feels like standing in a room with nothing left to hide behind, fully exposed, fully known, with no performance left to offer and no strategy left to execute.

That feeling is not a sign that something has gone wrong. That feeling is the sensation of a man finally arriving at the place where God can actually work, finally becoming the kind of availability that the repair requires, finally opening the crack that has been sealed against the gold for longer than the man can remember.

God has never been impressed by the performance. He has never been fooled by the management. He has been waiting with extraordinary patience and without a single moment of condemnation for the man to stop bringing the edited version of himself and bring the real one instead.

Proverbs 3:5-6 does not say, "Trust in the Lord and maintain a backup plan." It does not say, "Acknowledge Him in the areas where self-sufficiency has already proven insufficient while retaining personal authority over everything else." It says, "Trust in the Lord with all your heart, lean not on your own understanding, acknowledge Him in all your ways, and He will direct your paths."

The totality of that invitation is the entire point and the entire challenge. Not a partial surrender that releases the visible fractures while protecting the hidden ones. All of it. The marriage. The finances. The secret. The shame. The ambition. The fear. The identity. The future. Every crack, every fragment, every piece that a man has been gripping so tightly that his hands have gone numb around it, is placed fully and finally in the hands that are more than capable of doing something extraordinary with everything the man could not fix on his own.

There is a scene in the fifth chapter of John where Jesus approaches a man who has been lying at the pool of Bethesda for thirty-eight years, waiting for a healing that never came. Jesus asks him a question that sounds almost unnecessary, given the context. He asks whether the man wants to be made well.

The man's response is telling. He does not say yes. He explains why healing has been impossible, why every attempt has been defeated, and why the circumstances have consistently conspired against him. He gives Jesus his entire history of failed effort and calls it an answer to a question that required only a willingness to try one more time. Jesus, without addressing a single element of the explanation, tells him to rise, take up his mat, and walk.

The healing did not require the man's eloquence or his theological clarity or even a direct and unambiguous yes. It required his willingness to do what Jesus said in the moment Jesus said it. His obedience was his surrender, and his surrender was the crack opening and the gold entering and the healing walking through the only door it ever needed, which was the door of a man who finally stopped explaining why things could not change and simply allowed them to.

A man who surrenders to God does not become passive or irresponsible. He does not abdicate his role in his own life, his relationships, or his growth. What changes is not the level of his engagement but the source of his strength and the direction of his effort.

He stops spending his energy on the management of appearances and begins spending it on the genuine work of transformation. He becomes more intentional, not less. More honest with the people around him, not less. More present in his own life, not less.

A man who has nothing left to protect is free to be fully present in a way that a man still managing his image never can be. The surrender does not make him smaller. It makes him, maybe for the first time in his adult life, genuinely real. And a genuinely real man is a man whose cracks are open, whose gold is visible, and whose life is the kind of evidence that changes the atmosphere of every room he walks into.

The strength that emerges from genuine surrender is unlike anything a man produces through his own effort. It does not fluctuate with his circumstances. It does not evaporate when the pressure intensifies or when the people around him respond in ways he did not hope for. It is the strength Paul describes in Philippians 4, the ability to be content in every state, abased and abounding, full and hungry, because the source of the strength is not the circumstance but the God who is present in every circumstance without exception and who fills every crack that every circumstance produces with a gold that the circumstance itself could never provide.

That kind of strength cannot be manufactured through willpower, constructed through discipline, or built in any gym that exists. It can only be received. And it is only received through the open hands of a man who has finally stopped clenching his fists around a life he was never designed to carry alone and a crack he was never designed to seal by himself.

The Potter's hands have been reaching for you longer than you know. They have been reaching through every chapter of your breaking, through every season you misread as abandonment, through every moment the performance almost worked, and through every moment it did not. They have been reaching with the gold already prepared, already mixed, already exactly sufficient for every fracture in your life, no matter how deep, how wide, or how long it has been open.

Open yours. Place everything in His. And let Him work.

Chapter 9

MEN WHO WERE BROKEN AND STILL BUILT SOMETHING

Sitting in the middle of your own wreckage it is easy to conclude that the wreckage is the final word. That what has been broken cannot produce anything of lasting value. That the men who built things, who left marks, who changed the trajectory of families and communities and generations, were men who had it together in ways that you do not and perhaps never will. That temptation is one of the most effective lies the enemy deploys against a man in his lowest moments.

I want to dismantle that lie with evidence. Not with encouragement alone, though encouragement has its place. With the documented, unrevised, historically verified record of what God has done with broken men who made themselves available to Him despite everything their brokenness had produced and despite everything the enemy used that brokenness to tell them about themselves.

The record is not ambiguous; it is not a collection of exceptional cases that prove nothing about the general rule. It is the general rule. It is the consistent, repeated, and unmistakable pattern of a God who has always done His most significant work through men whose résumés, by human standards, should have disqualified them from the assignments they were given. Men whose cracks were wide, whose fractures were deep, and whose gold, when it finally appeared, was even more luminous because of the extent of the breaking that made room for it.

Moses spent the first forty years of his life in the palace of Pharaoh, educated and privileged and positioned by circumstances that appeared to be divine preparation for a great assignment. Then he killed a man, fled into the desert, and spent the next forty years as a shepherd in obscurity, tending another man's flock on the back side of a wilderness.

By the time God spoke to him from the burning bush, Moses was eighty years old. He was not the confident prince of Egypt who had once seemed destined for influence. He was a man who had lived so long in the shadow of his own failure that his first response to the call of God was a series of objections rooted in a self-assessment so diminished that he questioned whether he even could speak effectively in front of another human being.

The man standing before the burning bush was not impressive by any external measure. He was old, marked by his past, emptied of the confidence his early life had produced, and almost completely convinced that God had made a mistake in reaching for him. And God used him to deliver an entire nation from four hundred years of bondage.

The forty years in the wilderness did not disqualify Moses from his assignment. They were the precise preparation the assignment required, stripping away every false confidence, every form of self-reliance, every source of identity that was not rooted in God, until what remained was a man completely dependent on the God who was sending him. That is exactly the kind of man the mission needed. A man who still carried all the capability of his early formation, but who had been broken of every tendency to rely on that capability apart from God.

The crack that forty years of obscurity and failure produced in Moses was not the tragedy of his story. It was the specific fracture that God filled with the gold of humility and dependence that the palace never could have produced. And the gold in that crack was exactly what the deliverance of a nation required from the man who would lead it.

Peter is perhaps the most relatable broken man in the New Testament because his failure was so public, so specific, and so devastatingly close to the moment when his courage was needed most. He did not fail quietly or privately or in a season removed from his most important relationships. He denied Jesus three times in the span of a single night, in the courtyard of the high priest, while Jesus was being tried, within earshot of the very events his denial was abandoning. He failed at the worst possible moment in the most visible possible way, and then he went out and wept bitterly.

That detail matters, and I do not want to move past it too quickly. It tells us the depth of what Peter felt in the aftermath, that it was not the shallow embarrassment of a man who was momentarily caught off guard but the gut-level anguish of a man who understood exactly what he had done and could not find any way to undo it.

The crack that night produced in Peter was not a surface crack. It ran all the way down to the foundation of his identity, to the place where he had been most certain of himself, and it split that certainty open in the most public and painful way imaginable.

What Jesus did in response to that failure is one of the most intentional acts of restoration in all of Scripture. After the resurrection, He did not simply reinstate Peter to his previous position as though the denial had not happened. He did something more purposeful and more redemptive than erasure. He asked Peter three times if he loved Him; one question corresponding to each denial, giving Peter the specific opportunity to fill each crack with an affirmation, to speak gold into every place the denial had fractured.

Then, He gave Peter an assignment. Feed my sheep. Tend my lambs. The man who could not hold his confession together for a single night in a courtyard was given the responsibility of shepherding the early church into existence. Not because the denial was irrelevant but because the restoration was real, thorough, and gold-filled, and a man who has been restored by grace carries something in everything he does that a man who has never needed restoration simply does not possess. Peter's most powerful moments came after his most devastating failure because the grace that met him in that failure, and filled every crack the failure produced, was the very substance of the message he spent the rest of his life delivering.

Samson is a man whose story most people treat as a cautionary tale and nothing more. The caution in it is real and should not be dismissed. But there is something else in it for a man who is willing to look past the surface of the ending to what the ending actually produced.

Samson was a man of extraordinary gifting who made catastrophically poor choices, who allowed his appetites to override his anointing repeatedly, who told his secret to the wrong person, and lost everything that had made him significant in the eyes of the world around him. He ended up blind, bound, and grinding grain in a Philistine prison, a complete and humiliating inversion of everything he had been called to be.

Yet, in that prison, in the darkness and humiliation and complete stripping away of every external power he had ever relied upon, the crack of his total devastation became the surface through which God poured the most concentrated and consequential gold of his entire life. His hair began to grow again. The man who had spent his life relying on his own strength prayed one of the most honest prayers in Scripture. He asked God to remember him. Not to restore his reputation. Not to return him to prominence. Just to remember him. And God answered that prayer with a demonstration of power that exceeded anything Samson had produced during all the years of his self-reliant strength combined.

Paul carries the most dramatic transformation of any man in Scripture. I want to sit with it because it speaks directly to the man who believes his past is too specific, too dark, or too deliberately harmful to ever be redeemable by anything, including the grace of God. Paul was not a man who drifted into wrongdoing through weakness or circumstance. He was a man of conviction, intelligence, and religious zeal who directed all those qualities toward the systematic destruction of the early church.

He oversaw executions. He dragged men and women from their homes and delivered them to imprisonment and death. He was, by his own later admission, the chief of sinners, not a man who had merely fallen short but a man who had actively and zealously done damage that could not be undone by anything other than an extraordinary act of divine intervention. The crack in Paul's story was not produced by weakness. It was produced by willful and vigorous destruction. Yet, God met him on a road, called him by name, and redirected the full force of everything he was toward the very mission he had been trying to destroy.

What Paul built from that encounter is staggering in its scope and permanence. Letters written from prison cells that have shaped theology and transformed lives for two thousand years. Churches planted across continents that became the foundation of a movement that has never stopped expanding. A body of testimony about suffering and grace and purpose that remains the most articulate and personal expression of what God does with a broken and surrendered man that has ever been written.

None of it was possible without the breaking. Not just the dramatic breaking on the Damascus road but the ongoing breaking of a man who was constantly being pressed beyond his own capacity so that the power working through him would be unmistakably God and not Paul.

The gold running through every crack of Paul's life is so luminous and so extensive that two thousand years later, people are still being changed by the light it produces. The crack was total. The gold was complete. And the finished piece is still on display for every broken man who needs evidence that the repair is real.

The thread running through every one of these men is not that they were exceptional in their gifting or their character or their natural capacity for greatness. The thread is that God met them in their brokenness and did something through the encounter that neither the man nor any observer could have predicted from the outside.

Moses, the fugitive, became the deliverer. Peter, the denier, became the preacher of Pentecost. Samson, the compromised and humiliated judge, became the instrument of a victory his self-reliant years never produced. Paul, the persecutor, became the apostle whose influence has never stopped expanding across centuries and continents.

In every case, the breaking was real. In every case, the cost was significant. In every case, there was a season when the story felt finished and the crack looked permanent. And in every case, God proved that His assessment of a man's potential has never been based on the man's current condition, that the gold He prepared for a man's cracks was ready long before the man was willing to open them, and that the finished piece was always going to be more extraordinary than anything the original unbroken version could have become.

I want to say something directly to the man who has been carrying his wreckage, his shame, and his list of reasons why he is the exception or why his particular breaking is too extensive, too specific, or too self-inflicted to produce anything worth building on. You are not the exception. You have never been the exception.

You are exactly the kind of man God has always worked with; exactly the kind of material He has always chosen. He did not choose you in spite of the fractures but with full knowledge of every one of them. He has the gold already prepared for every crack in your life, no matter how deep it runs or how long it has been open.

The most celebrated Kintsugi pieces are not the ones that were barely chipped. They are the ones that were shattered completely, that looked beyond any reasonable hope of restoration, that the untrained eye would have dismissed without a second look. And what makes them extraordinary is not simply that someone repaired them. It is the extent of the gold.

The more complete the shattering, the more surface area there is for the gold to inhabit. The more extensive the fracture, the more luminous the finished piece becomes. And the more luminous the finished piece, the more undeniable the testimony of the Artist whose hands, whose gold, and whose patient and purposeful skill produced it.

You are not too broken to be used. You may be exactly broken enough for the kind of repair that produces the kind of gold that leaves people unable to explain what they are looking at apart from the grace and the power and the sovereign intention of the God who does not discard what He made, does not abandon what He started, and does not run out of gold for a single crack in a single life that has been placed in His hands.

Chapter 10

WHAT WOMEN NEED TO UNDERSTAND ABOUT BROKEN MEN

She has been watching him disappear for a long time. Not physically. He is still in the house, still at the table, still beside her at night. But something in him is absent in a way she cannot name and cannot seem to reach, and the harder she tries to close the distance, the wider it seems to become. She has not done anything wrong.

She is not the problem. She is standing at the edge of something that started long before she arrived in his life, something that was never about her, even when it was directed her way, something that has a name and a history and a God who is already working in it, even in seasons when that work is invisible to everyone, including her.

Most women who love broken men do not lack devotion. What they lack is language. They are watching something they cannot fully interpret, responding to symptoms they were never equipped to diagnose, and carrying the weight of confusion and quiet grief that nobody around them seems to understand.

She has prayed. She has waited. She has extended grace in ways that have cost her more than most people around her will ever know. And she is still standing, not because the weight has been light, but because something in her refuses to release the man she believes he was created to be.

She may not fully understand what she is actually looking at. A broken man does not present his brokenness cleanly. He does not sit down and explain that his father's absence left a wound that never healed, that the silence of his childhood taught him that emotions were liabilities, that every relationship he has entered has been quietly shaped by a fear of abandonment he could not articulate even if someone asked him directly.

He does not offer that transparency because, in most cases, he does not have access to it himself. What he offers instead is the translation of all that unprocessed pain into behavior. Withdrawal. Anger. Silence. Overwork. The compulsive reaching for something that temporarily quiets what he cannot bring himself to name.

A woman watching that behavior from the outside will almost always interpret it through the lens of her own experience. She will make it mean something about herself. About her adequacy. About her value. About whether she is enough for the man who is supposed to be her person. In almost every case, that interpretation, however understandable, is not what is actually happening.

When a man goes quiet in the middle of a conversation that requires emotional presence, he is rarely expressing indifference. He is experiencing something closer to overwhelm in a language he was never taught to speak.

The homes that produced most broken men were not places where emotional expression was modeled or safe. They were homes where a boy learned early that feelings were either ignored or penalized, where strength meant composure, and where the interior life was something managed privately and never brought into the open.

That boy grew into the man sitting across from her. And the silence she is reading as rejection is most often a man standing at the edge of something he does not know how to cross, wanting to reach her and having no bridge available that he knows how to build.

The wounds that formed him were real. This may be the most important truth a woman can carry into her love for a broken man. Whatever created the crack, whether it was a father who left, a mother whose love came with conditions attached, or trauma that rearranged his interior world before he had any framework for processing it, those things happened. They left marks.

Marks do not simply disappear because a man falls in love, makes a vow, or genuinely wants to be different. A wound does not heal because a man wills it closed. It heals because it is brought into the open, surrendered to God, and tended with patience and grace over enough time and enough consistency.

Most broken men have never experienced that kind of sustained grace from another person. Some of them have spent their entire lives quietly convinced that it does not exist for them.

A woman cannot be the source of a man's healing. That is a weight no human being was designed to carry and a responsibility that will deplete her if she accepts it as her own. The source of a broken man's healing is God, and the work that happens between a man and the God who made him is work that no other person can perform on his behalf.

A woman can create conditions where healing becomes more possible. She can speak to what is in him rather than only responding to what is coming out of him. She can pray with a precision that moves past the symptoms and goes directly to the wound beneath them. She can refuse to participate in the quiet agreement that keeps them both performing rather than genuinely connecting. She can hold the truth regarding who she knows him to be, even in the seasons when he cannot hold it for himself.

Ruth did not stay with Naomi because Naomi was easy to love. Naomi herself said there was nothing left worth staying for, that bitterness had taken everything joy once occupied, and that Ruth had every reasonable justification to return to what was familiar and uncomplicated. Ruth stayed because she had made a decision that was larger than the current condition of the person to whom she had made it.

That kind of love is not naive, and it is not without cost. It is the presence of a commitment that sees past the broken present into a future that only faith has the vision to access. There is some of that Ruth anointing available to every woman who refuses to let the hardest season write the final sentence of a story that God is still composing.

What a woman carries into her prayers for a broken man matters more than she may realize. When she prays past the behavior and into the wound, when she asks God to reach the place in him that she cannot reach, when she stands before God on behalf of a man who may not yet be standing there consistently for himself, she is participating in the repair in the most powerful way available to her. She is not the artist, but she is not absent from the work either.

The gold that fills a broken man's cracks does not always arrive only through his own surrender. Sometimes it comes through the intercession of a woman who loved him faithfully enough and long enough to keep bringing his name before the God who made him and has never once stopped knowing precisely where every crack runs and exactly how much gold it will require to fill it.

The patience required for loving a broken man is not manufactured through effort or sustained by emotion alone. It is the love Paul describes in 1 Corinthians 13, a love that bears all things and hopes all things and endures all things, a love that does not require the other person to be fully whole before it shows up fully present.

That kind of love is supernatural in its source because no woman has enough of it in her own reserves to sustain it indefinitely. It must come from God into her and through her before it reaches him. Which means the most important work she does for him is not always the work she does toward him. It is the work she does in her own relationship with God, keeping herself rooted, whole, and spiritually nourished so that what she pours into a broken man does not empty her in the process.

He may not be where he needs to be yet. The repair may be slower than she hoped and less visible than she prayed for. But slow is not stopped. And not yet is not never. God is doing something in the cracks that does not always announce itself before it is finished. The gold has been accumulating in places she cannot see, filling what her eyes have not yet been allowed to witness, making something out of this man and this story that neither of them could have become alone.

The Kintsugi artist works with patience that the broken piece cannot comprehend from the inside. The vessel does not feel the gold being poured. It simply holds still and trusts the hands it has been placed in. A woman who prays faithfully for a broken man is trusting those same hands with something she loves deeply. And those hands have never once dropped what has been placed in them.

Chapter 11

RAISING BOYS WHO WON'T BREAK THE SAME WAY

A repaired man does not get to keep his healing to himself. The moment a man begins to walk out of his own breaking, he discovers something he did not expect.

A boy is watching him. A son. A nephew. A young man in his circle. And that boy is building his entire definition of manhood from everything he sees in the man standing closest to him.

He understands that what he does now, how he lives now, what he models and says and makes room for and refuses to tolerate in himself, is not just about him anymore. It never was. But he can see that clearly now in a way he could not see it when he was still in the middle of his own wreckage.

A repaired man carries a responsibility that an unbroken man never fully comprehends. A repaired man knows exactly what the breaking costs and exactly what the gold required He also knows exactly what it means to pass either one of those things forward to the next generation.

The cycle that produced his pain did not begin with him. He received it from a man who received it from the man before him, passed down through bloodlines and households and patterns of silence and absence and unaddressed wounds that nobody ever stopped long enough to name.

Generational brokenness does not announce itself as an inheritance. It arrives disguised as normal.

The boy who grows up watching his father manage emotions with anger does not think he is learning a broken pattern. He thinks he is learning what men do. The boy who never sees his father cry does not think he is being taught that grief is shameful. He thinks he is learning what strength looks like. The boy whose father is physically present but emotionally unreachable does not think he is experiencing a form of abandonment. He thinks that distant is simply what fathers are. When that boy becomes a man, and he does what men do, and he is what strength looks like, and he keeps the distance that fathers keep, the cycle moves forward one more generation without anyone ever having chosen it deliberately.

One man who decides to do the work can end what has been moving through a family for generations. That is not a small thing. That is one of the most significant acts available to a repaired man, and it does not require a platform or a title or a formal role. It requires presence. It requires honesty. It requires the willingness to be a different kind of man in front of a boy who is watching everything and absorbing everything and building his entire internal architecture of what manhood means from what he sees in the man closest to him.

Deuteronomy 6 tells fathers to teach their children diligently, to speak of God's truth when sitting in the house and walking on the road and lying down and rising up. The image is not of formal instruction, nor a scheduled curriculum delivered at appointed times. It is the image of a life being lived openly in front of children, of truth woven into ordinary moments, of a man whose daily existence is itself the lesson.

What a boy needs from the man in his life is not a perfect man. He has never needed that, and he will not find it. What he needs is an honest one. A man who lets him see that struggle is real, that God is present in the struggle, and that the combination of those two truths is not a contradiction but the very foundation of a life that can hold weight.

A healed man gives a boy permission to feel. This is more significant than it sounds because most boys are receiving the opposite permission from every direction available to them. They are told in a hundred subtle and not-so-subtle ways that emotion is weakness, that vulnerability is risk, that the appropriate response to pain is to absorb it quietly and keep moving.

Boys learn that lesson not primarily from what they are told, but from what they observe. A father who never cries in front of his son is teaching his son something. A father who processes every difficulty through silence or anger or withdrawal is passing a curriculum forward whether he intends to or not.

However, a man who has been broken and repaired, who has learned in the most personal and costly way possible that emotions denied do not disappear but simply go underground and do damage from below, that man has something to offer a boy that no amount of instruction can replace. He can model what it looks like to feel something real and bring it to God and remain standing. He can let the boy see that grief and strength are not opposites. That a man can weep and still lead. That bringing your interior life before God is not the abandonment of courage but the highest expression of it.

David gave Solomon something that most men never give their sons. He gave him honesty about the interior life. The Psalms that David wrote were not private documents kept hidden from the people around him. They were the record of a man's real experience with God, the fear and the doubt and the gratitude and the grief and the wonder, all of it laid out without the editing that pride demands.

Solomon grew up knowing that his father was a man who felt things deeply and brought those feelings to God without shame. That did not make Solomon immune to his own failures, and his story carries its own weight of broken places. But the inheritance David gave him was real and it was honest and it pointed toward a God who was large enough to hold everything a man carried without requiring him to carry it alone.

A repaired man mentors differently than a man who has never been broken. He listens with a depth that comes from having needed someone to listen to him in the way nobody did. He speaks into a young man's life without the false confidence of a man who has never failed, which means what he says carries the credibility of someone who has been in the place he is describing.

He does not need the boy to perform for him because he has been freed from the exhaustion of performance himself. He can sit with a young man in the middle of a mess and not flinch and not fix prematurely and not communicate through his discomfort that the mess is too much. Because he has been in a mess and he knows that the presence of someone who does not run from it is one of the most powerful gifts one man can give another.

Psalm 78 says to tell the next generation the praiseworthy deeds of the Lord, the things He has done. It does not say to protect the next generation from the knowledge of how difficult the journey was. It says to tell them what God did in it.

The testimony of a repaired man is not just his current wholeness. It is the full account of the breaking and the surrender and the slow, painful, faithful process of the mending and the God who was present in every stage of it without exception.

A boy who hears that testimony from a man he respects does not just receive information. He receives permission. Permission to be honest about his own breaking when it comes. Permission to bring it to God rather than seal it against the world. Permission to believe that the crack in his life is not the end of his story but the beginning of the most significant part of it.

There is a promise in Malachi 4 that the hearts of fathers will turn to their children and the hearts of children to their fathers. That turning is not automatic. It requires a man who has done enough of his own healing to have something to turn to.

A man who is still sealed against his own pain cannot genuinely open toward his son, no matter how much he loves him, because access to another person's interior life requires a man to have access to his own first. The repair that God does in a man is never only for that man. It moves. It spreads. It changes the temperature of a home and the atmosphere of a relationship, and the inheritance of a child who may never be able to articulate what is different about the man raising him, but who will carry the difference into every significant relationship of his adult life.

The boy watching you right now is building his definition of manhood from what he sees in you. Not from what you tell him. From what he sees.

He is watching how you handle failure. He is watching whether you apologize when you are wrong. He is watching how you speak to his mother and whether you keep your word, and whether you show up when it is inconvenient and whether the God you say you believe in is someone you actually go to when things are hard or someone you only mention in comfortable circumstances. He is watching all of it and filing all of it away. It is becoming the foundation on which he will build his own life and his own relationships and his own understanding of what a man is supposed to be.

You cannot give him what you have not allowed God to produce in you. But what God has produced in you, the gold that runs through every crack of your repaired life, is something no school and no program and no amount of good intention can replicate. It is the specific and irreplaceable testimony of a man who was broken and surrendered and mended, and it is exactly what the boy in your life needs to see more than anything else you could offer him.

The cycle ends when a repaired man decides it ends. Not through perfection. Through honesty. Through presence. Through the willingness to be the first man in his line who lets the boy see the gold and know where it came from and understand that the God who filled those cracks is the same God who is already reaching for every crack that boy will ever have in his own life.

That is the inheritance worth leaving. Not the absence of breaking. The evidence that the breaking is never the final word.

Chapter 12

THE MASTERPIECE

(WALKING IN YOUR REPAIRED IDENTITY)

You are not who you were when you opened this book. Something has moved. Something that was sealed has been opened. Something that had no name has been given one.

The man sitting with these pages is a man who has been in the presence of a truth that does not release you the same way it found you. This truth has been working in the cracks of everything he brought to this reading even when he was not fully aware that the work was happening.

This chapter is not a summary. It is not a list of principles to carry forward or a checklist of commitments to make before closing the cover. It is a commissioning. It is the moment the artist sets down his tools, steps back from the work, and the vessel that was broken and brought and surrendered and slowly, carefully, intentionally repaired is lifted into the light for the first time in its completed form.

What the light reveals is not what the vessel was before it broke. It is something more. Something that could not have existed without the breaking. Something that carries in every golden seam the full testimony of what it cost and what it took and who was present through every stage of the repair and whose hands did what no other hands were qualified to do.

A repaired man is not a man who has returned to who he was before things went wrong. That man is gone, and he is not coming back, and that is not a loss worth grieving. The man who existed before the breaking was a man whose cracks had not yet been filled with gold, whose fractures had not yet been touched by the hands of God, whose identity was built on foundations that the breaking eventually proved were not sufficient to hold the full weight of the life he was called to live.

The man who emerges from genuine surrender and genuine repair is not a restoration of that original version. He is something new. Something stronger at the broken places than he ever was before they broke. Something that bears in his very structure the evidence of a grace that is more powerful than any damage life has been able to produce.

Isaiah 61 opens with the declaration that the Spirit of the Lord is upon a man to bind up the brokenhearted, to proclaim liberty to captives, to give beauty for ashes and the oil of joy for mourning and a garment of praise for a spirit of heaviness. Every exchange in that passage moves in the same direction. What was destroyed is replaced by something living. What was heavy is lifted by something light. What was ash is transformed into something beautiful.

The man standing on the other side of that exchange is not diminished by what it cost him to get there. He is defined by what God gave him in the place of what the breaking took. The ashes were real. The beauty is more real. And the man wearing it carries both truths simultaneously in a way that makes his life a testimony that requires no explanation beyond the evidence of what is visibly different about him.

Walking in a repaired identity is not a performance of wholeness. It is not the construction of a new and more sophisticated version of the same management that kept the cracks sealed for years. A man who has genuinely been through the process of surrender and repair does not need to perform his healing because his healing is not a presentation.

It is a reality that is present in the room before he says a word about it. It is in the way he listens without needing to fix immediately. It is in the way he can sit with another man's pain without flinching because he has sat with his own. It is in the way he leads from a place of strength rather than the anxious energy of a man who is still afraid of being found out. It is in the way he loves his wife or his children or the people in his circle with a presence and patience that were not available to him when he was still spending all his energy on the maintenance of his own sealed fractures.

Philippians 1:6 says He who began a good work in you will carry it on to completion until the day of Christ Jesus. That verse is not primarily about what a man does going forward. It is about who is doing the continuing work.

The God who reached into the breaking and poured in the gold does not stop at a certain level of repair and hand the project back to the man to finish on his own. The work is ongoing. The gold is still being applied in places that have not yet fully opened.

There are cracks in every man's life that have not yet been fully surrendered; areas where the grip is still tight and the sealing is still active. The commitment of God to that man's completion is not contingent on the man's speed or his consistency or his ability to get it right on the first attempt. What is required of the man is not perfection. What is required is continued availability. Continued openness. The same surrender that began the repair extended as a daily posture rather than a single dramatic moment.

A repaired man reads his own story differently than a broken man does. The broken man looks at his past and sees evidence of his inadequacy, a record of failures and fractures that confirms every fear he has ever carried about his own worth and his own capacity.

The repaired man looks at the same past and sees something else entirely. He sees the fingerprints of a God who was present in every chapter, including the ones that looked like abandonment. He sees the through line of a sovereign hand that was working even in the seasons that felt like waste, that was preparing even in the seasons that felt like punishment, that was never surprised by a single thing that happened and never once revised His assessment of what the finished piece was going to become. The past does not change, but the lens through which a repaired man sees it changes everything about what it means and everything it is allowed to produce going forward.

Revelation 21 says He makes all things new. Not repairs all things to their original condition. Makes them new. The newness is the point.

The vessel that comes out of the Kintsugi process is not the vessel that went in. It is a new thing that contains the history of the old thing transformed by the gold that runs through every place the old thing was broken.

A repaired man carries his history. He does not hide it and he does not lead with it as a badge he needs people to validate. He carries it the way a man carries a scar that no longer hurts, with the quiet knowledge of what it cost and the even quieter knowledge of who healed it and what the healing proved about the God who was present through the entire process from the first crack to the final seam.

There are people in a repaired man's path who will be changed by what they encounter in him before he ever opens his mouth about what God has done because the gold is visible. It is not hidden in a healed man who is walking in his repaired identity. It shows in his stability. It shows in his compassion. It shows in the way he does not require the people around him to manage his emotions for him, protect him from the truth, or perform for his approval. It shows in the way he can be fully present in a moment of crisis without the crisis swallowing him, because he has already been through the fire that he once feared most and he came out of it not destroyed, but refined.

1 Peter 1 says that genuine faith proven through fire comes out more precious than gold. The man who has been through the breaking, the surrender, and the slow, faithful repair is not a man to be pitied. He is a man whose proven faith is on display in a way that untested faith simply cannot replicate. The scars are not shameful. They are the sermon.

Every place the gold runs in a repaired man's life is a line of testimony that points directly to the God whose grace was sufficient for that specific fracture in that specific man at that specific moment. A man who walks in his repaired identity does not need to manufacture a message. He is the message. The way he fathers, loves, leads, handles failure now compared to how he handled it before, the way he can speak into another man's breaking with the authority of someone who has been there and knows the way through—all of it is the gold made visible. All of it is the work of the artist on display in the life of the vessel He refused to discard.

You were not too broken to be repaired. You were not too far gone for the gold to reach. You were not the exception to the pattern God demonstrated through every broken man He has ever worked with from the beginning of recorded history until now. You were exactly what He was looking for. A man with cracks deep enough, wide enough, and honest enough to finally open to the only hands that were ever qualified to fill them.

What He has made of you and what He is still making of you is not a lesser version of what you might have been if you had never broken. It is greater. It is more honest. It is more useful. It is more capable of reaching the man sitting in his own darkness who needs to see evidence that the repair is real before he will risk believing it is available for him.

Walk in it. Not in the performance of it; the reality of it. Walk in the daily surrender that keeps the gold fresh and the cracks open to whatever the artist still wants to pour. Walk in the identity of a man who has been broken, found, filled, commissioned, and sent back into the world; not despite his fractures but because of what God put in them.

The masterpiece is not what it was before it broke. It is greater. It is golden. And it is complete.

Conclusion

THE GOLD DOES NOT LIE

I want to talk to you one more time before you finish this book. Not as an author wrapping up a project but as a man who has walked through his own breaking, who has sat in his own rubble, who has carried his own archive of things he never intended to show anyone, and who has discovered on the other side of surrender that everything God promised about what He does with broken pieces is exactly and completely true.

I did not write these chapters from a comfortable distance. I wrote them from the interior of a life that has known the specific weight of the things described in every one of them. What I know with a certainty that no amount of argument or discouragement has ever been able to shake is that the God who met me at my breaking is the same God who has been present in yours, and that the gold He poured into my cracks is the same gold He has been preparing for every fracture in your life since before you were born.

The Japanese artist who first looked at a shattered piece of pottery and decided to repair it with gold instead of discarding it understood something that most of the world had not yet grasped. He understood that the history of a broken thing does not diminish its value. He understood that the crack is not the enemy of beauty but the very place where beauty, of the most striking and permanent kind, becomes possible. He understood that the finished piece, the one with gold running through every fracture, visible, luminous, and impossible to ignore, is worth more than the original ever was. Not despite what it went through. Because of it. The breaking was not the tragedy of the vessel's story. The breaking was the beginning of its most important chapter.

That is your story. Not a story of a man who was broken and survived it. A story of a man who was broken and was found by a God who specializes in the kind of repair that makes the finished piece more extraordinary than anything the original wholeness could have produced.

Every chapter of this book has been an attempt to name something that God has been doing in the lives of men since the first man drew breath and found himself in need of more than his own resources could provide. The crack in the garden. The crack in the pit. The crack in the prison. The crack in the wilderness. The crack in the courtyard where a man denied the One he loved most. God has been meeting men in their cracks and filling them with gold for as long as men have been breaking, and He has never once run out of either the patience or the gold to do it.

I want to speak to the different men who are holding this book as these closing words are being read. There is the man who came to these pages already in the middle of his breaking, who started the introduction with nothing left to lose, and who has read every chapter with the specific recognition of a man seeing his own story described with an accuracy he did not expect. To that man, I want to say that what you felt while reading was not a coincidence.

God does not allow a man to encounter truth at the level of his soul without intention. The recognition you experienced, the places where something landed in your chest with a weight that you knew was real, those were not literary moments. Those were the Potter's reaching for your pieces.

He is not reaching from a distance. He is right there, in whatever room you are sitting in, closer than the breath you just took, more committed to your restoration than you have ever been able to be on your own. You do not have to have a plan. You do not have to have a prayer that sounds right. You only have to open your hands and stop gripping what you were never designed to hold alone.

There is the man who came to these pages already in process, already somewhere in the middle of the repair, who recognized in these chapters the language for things he has been experiencing but could not fully articulate. The surrender that felt like loss but produced unexpected freedom. The crack that he finally stopped sealing and found, to his own amazement, that God was already there when it opened. The relationships that are slowly filling with something more honest and durable than what was there before the breaking. To that man, I want to say, keep going. The work God began in you is not finished.

The chapters still ahead are not a threat to what He has already done. They are the continuation of it, and every crack that still needs gold is a place where more of His presence is about to become visible in your life. Do not grow impatient with the process.

The Kintsugi artist does not rush. Every crack is filled with the care and intentionality of a craftsman who knows exactly what the finished piece is going to look like and who is unwilling to compromise the quality of the repair for the sake of speed.

There is the man who almost did not pick up this book, or who almost put it down in the early chapters because the honesty was uncomfortable. The distance between who he is and who these pages describe felt too great to navigate. If that man is still reading, if he made it all the way to this part of the book despite the discomfort, doubt, and the internal resistance that broken men carry into every space that threatens to see them clearly, then I want him to know that the fact that he is still here is itself significant.

God does not let a man read to the end of an invitation without reason. Your arrival at this place is not accidental. It is the end of a conversation that God started before the book was ever opened, and the question He is asking is not complicated. It does not require a theological framework or a history of religious commitment to answer. It only requires honesty.

Are you willing to let the Potter have the pieces? All of them? The ones you are ashamed of. The ones that were done to you. The ones that have been sitting in the archive so long that you have stopped believing they could ever be anything other than what they are. Are you willing to open your hands?

There is the woman who read every chapter and recognized the men in her life in ways that were sometimes painful, sometimes clarifying, and sometimes both at once. She arrived at these final pages with a more complete picture of what she has been watching and living alongside than she had when she began. To her, I want to say that what she carries in intercession for the broken men in her life is not wasted.

God hears every prayer spoken over a man who does not yet know he needs it. He honors every act of faithful presence offered to a man who has not yet learned how to receive it. And the understanding she has gained, the ability to see the wound beneath the behavior and the crack beneath the performance, is itself a form of gold. It makes her love more targeted, more effective, and more aligned with what God is already doing in a broken man's life than frustration alone could ever be.

And there is the man who read these pages and felt nothing, whose crack is sealed so tightly and has been sealed for so long that the truth described in every chapter slid off the surface without finding an opening. I refuse to believe that man does not exist, because I have been that man, and the sealing that feels like strength is the most complete and costly form of brokenness there is. To that man, I want to say simply that God is not finished with him either.

The same sovereignty that broke Job and Joseph and Moses and Peter and Paul and every other man in these pages who looked for a season like he was beyond reaching is the same sovereignty that is present in the life of a man whose crack is still sealed. The Potter is patient in a way that outlasts even the most determined resistance.

The gold is still prepared. It will wait as long as it needs to wait. Because what God makes, He does not abandon. And what He intends to fill, He will fill, in His time, in His way, with a precision and beauty that no amount of prior resistance will be able to diminish.

There are things I know now that I did not know in the seasons of my own breaking. I know that the silence of God is not the absence of God. I know that the crack that feels like it is ending you is the very place He has been planning to meet you since before you were born.

I know that the gold He pours into a surrendered man's fractures is not decorative. It is structural. It makes the repaired place stronger than the original surface ever was, more capable of bearing weight, more resistant to the pressures that shattered the original, and more luminous under every kind of light.

I know that the man who comes out of the Kintsugi process is not a diminished version of who he was before the breaking. He is the version the breaking made possible, carrying something in his cracked and golden places that no unbroken man can replicate, speaking with an authority that only comes from having been through something and having found God sufficient in the middle of it.

The gold does not lie. It never has. Every place in a man's life where God has done the work of genuine repair, where the surrender was real, the process was honest, and the Potter was allowed to do what only the Potter can do.

The gold is visible. It does not fade. It does not rust. It does not diminish with the passing of time or the accumulation of new pressures. It remains. Permanent, luminous, and impossible to explain apart from the hands that placed it there.

The man who carries it, who walks through the world with gold visible in his cracks, is not just a healed man. He is a testimony. A living, breathing, undeniable argument that the God who repairs broken things is real, that His gold is genuine, and that no piece is too shattered for His hands to restore.

You are that piece. You have always been that piece. The hands that have been reaching for you through every chapter of this book, through every season of your life that these pages have named, addressed, and pointed toward grace; those hands have not moved. They are exactly where they have always been. Closer than your next breath. More patient than your longest silence. More committed to the finished picture than you have ever been able to be on your own.

Place what you are carrying in those hands. Every crack. Every fragment. Every piece you have been gripping so long that you have forgotten what it felt like to let go. Place it all in those hands and watch what the Potter does with what the world, and sometimes you yourself, had already decided was beyond repair.

The gold does not lie. And neither does the God who made it, prepared it, and has been waiting to pour it into every broken place in your life since before you had the first crack to fill.

KINTSUGI MAN

DISCUSSION GUIDE

A Note Before You Begin

These questions are not designed to be answered quickly. They are designed to be answered honestly. Whether you are working through this book alone, with another man, or in a group setting, resist the temptation to give the answer that sounds right and give the answer that is true instead.

The gold cannot fill what you are not willing to open. That is as true in a conversation as it is in a life.

Chapter 1

BROKEN BEFORE YOU KNEW YOUR NAME

- What is one thing you inherited from your family of origin, a pattern, a silence, or a wound, that you carried into your adult life without ever choosing it?

- When you look at the man your father was, what did he model for you about how a man handles pain? How has that shaped the way you handle it?

- Have you ever considered that some of what broke you was not your fault? What does it feel like to sit with that honestly?

- What would it mean for you personally to believe that God saw every chapter of your early life and was already at work in it?

Chapter 2

STRONG MEN DON'T CRY

- Where did you first learn that showing emotion was a weakness? Who taught you that, and did they know they were teaching it?

- What emotion do you find most difficult to express, and what do you do with it instead of expressing it?

- Jesus wept. David wept. What does it do to your defintion of strength to sit with that truth?

- What is one thing you have been carrying in silence that you have never brought to God or another person out loud?

Chapter 3

THE WEIGHT OF WHAT YOUR'E CARRYING

- What is the heaviest thing you are carrying right now that you have not fully surrendered to God?

- Shame tells a man he is what he has done. How has shame shaped the way you see yourself and the way you move through the world?

- Is there something in your past that you have convinced yourself disqualifies you? What would it mean to lay that specific thing down?

- What would your life look like if you actually believed that God's grace was sufficient for the exact thing you are most ashamed of?

Chapter 4

WHEN GOD DOES THE BREAKING

- Has there been a season in your life that felt like God was absent or even working against you? Looking back, what do you see now that you could not see then?

- How do you tend to respond when God allows something painful? Do you pull away from Him or move toward Him?

- Job, Joseph, and Paul all went through seasons that made no sense from the inside. Which of their stories connects most with where you are right now, and why?

- What would it require of you to trust a God who permits breaking as part of His process?

Chapter 5

THE WOUNDS THAT SHAPED YOU

- If you had to name your deepest wound, the one that has most consistently affected your relationships and your sense of self, what would you name it?

- What is the difference between a wound that has shaped you and a wound that is still controlling you? Which category does your deepest wound fall into right now?

- Have you ever brought that wound specifically and honestly before God? Not in general terms, but with its actual name and its actual cost?

- 2 Corinthians 12 says God's strength is made perfect in weakness. What would it look like for your specific weakness to become the place where His strength is most visible?

Chapter 6

BROKEN RELATIONSHIPS AND THE MEN WHO GAVE UP

- Is there a relationship in your life—a marriage, a child, a friend, or a brother—that your brokenness has damaged? What has it cost both of you?

- What is the difference between genuine reconciliation and cheap reconciliation? Which one have you been reaching for?

- What would it require of you to become a different man in that relationship, not to fix what is broken overnight but to begin moving in a different direction?

- Joel two and twenty-five says God will restore the years the locusts have eaten. Do you believe that is available for the specific relationship you are thinking about right now?

Chapter 7

THE CRISIS OF PURPOSE

- On a scale of one to ten, how clearly can you articulate what you were created to do? What keeps that number from being higher?

- What has purposelessness cost you? Where has the absence of direction shown up most destructively in your life?

- Ephesians two and ten says you are God's workmanship, created for good works He prepared in advance. What would it mean to actually live from that identity rather than just acknowledge it?

- What is one step, however small, that you could take this week toward the assignment you know God has placed on your life?

Chapter 8

THE MENDING

- What does the word surrender mean to you, honestly? Not theologically. In your gut, when you hear that word, what do you feel?

- Where in your life are you still gripping the broken pieces and trying to arrange them yourself instead of placing them in God's hands?

- The man at the pool of Bethesda spent thirty-eight years explaining why healing was impossible. What explanations have you been giving God for why your situation cannot change?

- What would genuine surrender look like for you specifically this week? Not in general. In the actual circumstances of your actual life right now.

Chapter 9

MEN WHO WERE BROKEN AND STILL BUILT SOMETHING

- Which of the men in this chapter, Moses, Peter, Samson, or Paul, do you most identify with, and why?

- What has your breaking produced in you that your unbroken years never could have? Take your time with this one.

- Have you been using your past as evidence that you are disqualified? What would it mean to let God reframe that same past as preparation instead?

- Who in your circle needs to hear your testimony right now? What is keeping you from telling it?

Chapter 10

WHAT WOMEN NEED TO UNDERSTAND ABOUT BROKEN MEN

- If the woman who loves you most could see clearly what is happening inside you right now, what would she see that she does not currently have language for?

- How has your brokenness affected the way you receive love? Do you push it away, perform for it, or something else?

- What is one thing you wish the woman in your life understood about you that you have never found the words to tell her?

- What would it look like to let her into the repair process rather than managing what she sees of it?

Chapter 11

RAISING BOYS WHO WON'T BREAK THE SAME WAY

- What are you currently passing forward to the next generation, intentionally or unintentionally, that you received from the generation before you?

- Is there a boy or young man in your life who is watching you right now? What is he learning about manhood from what he sees?

- What is one thing you needed from a man when you were young that you did not receive? How can you give that specific thing to the next generation?

- What does breaking the cycle actually require of you, practically, not in theory, but in the specific relationships and responsibilities you carry right now?

Chapter 12

THE MASTERPIECE

- Looking back over this book and over your own story, where do you see gold that you previously saw only as damage?

- What has changed in the way you see yourself between the first chapter and this one? Be specific.

- A repaired man's scars are his sermon. What is your sermon? What does your specific story say about the grace and power of God?

- What is the one thing you are going to do differently starting today because of what God has been saying to you through these pages?

A FINAL WORD TO EVERY MAN WHO MADE IT TO THIS PAGE

You did not finish this book by accident. Something in you was willing to stay with the hard questions and the honest pages and the truth that does not always feel comfortable before it feels true. That willingness is itself the gold beginning to show.

Keep going. Keep surrendering. Keep bringing every crack to the hands that have never once run out of gold for a man who is willing to open them. The masterpiece is not finished. But it is well underway.

Made in the USA
Coppell, TX
18 July 2026

84536109R00079